#
AF265002

These stories identify the sins of youth,
relate the times I cried out for God,
describe the good and perfects gift given from the Father,
explain the need for purification,
and the wonder and excitement of revelation.

I explain how I was rescued,
engaged in spiritual warfare,
made it out of Egypt,
through the wilderness, and
across the Jordan.

These stories relate the blessings of giving gifts,
receiving gifts,
and promises through prophecy.
We have a blessed assurance of our future,
including expansion and increase.

God created us to be strong and courageous
so that we may proclaim the Cross
with wisdom and understanding,
speak life into others,
and feed His little lambs.

HIS CHILD

Asking Jesus for Your True Identity

SAMANTHA HARRELL

His Child: Asking Jesus for Your True Identity
Copyright 2020 by Samantha Harrell

All rights reserved. No part of this book may be reproduced, stored in a retrieval system, or transmitted in any form or by any means-electronic, mechanical, photocopy, recording, or otherwise-without prior written permission of the copyright owner. Names of some people in this book have been changed to protect their identity.

Scripture quotations marked TPT are from *The Passion Translation*®. Copyright © 2017, 2018 by Passion & Fire Ministries, Inc. Used by permission. All rights reserved. ThePassionTranslation.com.

Scripture quotations marked (NIV) are taken from the *Holy Bible, New International Version*®, NIV®. Copyright © 1973, 1978, 1984, 2011 by Biblica, Inc.™ Used by permission of Zondervan. All rights reserved worldwide. www.zondervan.comThe "NIV" and "New International Version" are trademarks registered in the United States Patent and Trademark Office by Biblica, Inc.™

Scripture quotations marked (ESV) are from the ESV® Bible (*The Holy Bible, English Standard Version*®), copyright © 2001 by Crossway, a publishing ministry of Good News Publishers. Used by permission. All rights reserved.

Scripture quotations marked (NLT) are taken from *the Holy Bible, New Living Translation*, copyright ©1996, 2004, 2015 by Tyndale House Foundation. Used by permission of Tyndale House Publishers, a Division of Tyndale House Ministries, Carol Stream, Illinois 60188. All rights reserved.

Scripture quotations marked (NKJV) are taken from the *New King James Version*®. Copyright © 1982 by Thomas Nelson. Used by permission. All rights reserved.

Scripture quotations taken from the *Amplified*® Bible (AMP), Copyright © 2015 by The Lockman Foundation. Used by permission. www.Lockman.org

Scripture quotations marked (TLB) are taken from The Living Bible copyright © 1971. Used by permission of Tyndale House Publishers, a Division of Tyndale House Ministries, Carol Stream, Illinois 60188. All rights reserved.

All emphasis in scripture is author's own.

Editing credits:
    Cathy Sanders
    Rhonda Fleming

Interior Design credit:
    Cathy Sanders

Cover Design credits:
    Nicholas Harrell
    Cathy Sanders

ISBN: 978-0-578-64166-9 (Print)
           978-0-578-64272-7 (E-book)

Printed in the USA.

To Jesus, The Author and Redeemer, my first love and
primary inspiration.

To Nick, Jackson, Charles, Evelyn, and Nick Jr. You're
the lights of my life. Thank you for inspiring so much
of this book. God bless you always. I love you.

Contents

Acknowledgments

Thanks to my parents for your support and the wonderful gift of life. God bless you always. I love you.

Thanks to my grandmother, aunt, and Nick's parents (my in-laws) for your continued support and encouragement. God bless you always. I love you.

Thanks to Britta and Zaina for your timely prophetic messages of love and hope. God bless you always.

Thanks to my editors, Rhonda and Cathy (also the designer) for your talents, thoughtfulness, encouragement, and beautiful blessings. God bless you always.

Thanks to everyone else who was mentioned in or otherwise contributed to these stories. God bless you always!

Introduction

God has special plans for each of us that are more wonderful and exciting than we can imagine (1 Corinthians 2:9). I pray this book helps you find His path for your life and realize you are not alone on the journey. He is always with you. Other people have been where you are and watched in awe as God lifted them above their circumstances to a place of victory. From your trials you will emerge with the crown of life, which God has promised those who love him (James 1:12). I pray these stories bless you and that one day you'll have your own collection of stories to share about God's goodness and saving grace. This book can be used as a daily devotional. Each of my "God stories" includes encouragement for you, biblical truth from God's Word, and a closing prayer.

God's plan for me has proved to be more exciting and fulfilling than I could have dreamt. He had a full life planned for me, even though it took me many years to accept it and begin down the path of joy and freedom in the Lord. He sets before all of us life and death, blessings and curses, and asks us to choose life with Him (Deuteronomy 30:19-20). His plan for you is perfect and beautiful. He's just waiting for you to accept His love and forgiveness.

Jesus intervened in my life at a moment during young adulthood when I needed help choosing Him. He showed me the difference between life and death and assured me it wasn't too late to change course onto the path of true beauty and fruitfulness. He gives each of us the freedom to choose, but like a good father, He also gives us lots of hints and encouragement along the way regarding the best path to take. This book will help you understand who God is and what He wants for you. Perhaps you'll identify with some of my struggles and victories and be inspired to place your hope in the Lord. God bless you!

Introduction

Part 1:

Redemption/Adoption

I will be a true Father to you, and you will be my beloved sons and daughters, says the Lord Yahweh Almighty.

2 Corinthians 6:18 TPT

Separation

Before you were saved, you probably didn't have a relationship with our Creator. You may have ignored Him, been angry at Him, or even denied His existence. Even people who are brought up in Christian homes tend to wander away from God at some point. Perhaps you're still not sure where you stand with Him. I want you to know that it's never too late to return to Him or to ask Him into your life for the very first time.

> For this reason the Lord is still waiting to show his favor to you so he can show you his marvelous love. He waits to be gracious to you. He sits on his throne ready to show mercy to you. For Yahweh is the Lord of justice, faithful to keep his promises. Overwhelmed with bliss are all who will entwine their hearts in him, waiting for him to help them (Isaiah 30:18 TPT).

I went through my childhood and young adulthood without knowing our wonderful Creator, the Lord Jesus. I visited church occasionally, was baptized, and went through the motions of a religious life, but I didn't know how to give and receive love because I didn't know God. He is love (1 John 4:8). I had few friends, no siblings, and pushed almost everyone away who tried to be kind to me. I'm sure this grieved the Lord because He didn't create us to live in isolation (Genesis 2:18).

When I was in school I often chose to surround myself with people who were unkind to me because I thought that was how popular kids were supposed to act. Unfortunately, they weren't the kind of people who would lead me to God and, unsurprisingly, I spent most of my school days in misery. If the guy I liked or the girl I wanted to befriend didn't happen to feel the same way about me, I would spiral into a black pit of despair. In one day I could go from seeing myself as beautiful in the morning to hating myself by the time I came home from school. I was seeking the love I needed from people who didn't know God. Rejection was my constant companion—until I asked God for help.

I've heard that during a near-death experience, the Lord may ask a person if they have learned to love. If the answer is no, He may send them back to life for a second chance. Fortunately, most of us won't have to die and go to heaven before we learn to love and receive love well. I pray we all experience God's goodness in the land of the living (Psalm 27:13). If you're in a dark and lonely place, know that our heavenly Father is waiting on you to ask Him for help. When you do, you'll receive His forgiveness, companionship, help, wisdom, and blessings. God's Word says:

> And it's true: "Everyone who calls on the name of the Lord Yahweh will be rescued and experience new life" (Romans 10:13 TPT).

> *Dear Lord Jesus, please live in my heart and guide my life. Show me the truth, what I need to change, and how to love. Forgive me for the wrongdoing that causes me so much guilt, and please forgive the people who cause me so much pain. Help me to forgive others as You've forgiven me so I can walk in the freedom You paid for. Show me my destiny and how to get there, and help me appreciate Your blessings along the way. Thank You for Your sacrifice and protection. In Your holy name I pray, amen.*

Heartbreak

If you're human, then you've suffered a broken heart at some point. If the pain is great enough, it may seem as if your heart will never mend. I believe Jesus' heart was broken when He lived among us. He was rejected in his hometown (Matthew 13:54-58), betrayed by his friends, and mocked, beaten, and discarded by those He loved and came to save. Whatever you're going through, the Lord knows how you hurt. He's been there. Trust that He didn't cause your pain and wants to heal you to give you a fresh start.

> The Lord is close to all whose hearts are crushed by pain, and he is always ready to restore the repentant one (Psalm 34:18 TPT).

A person's first heartbreak can set a devastating course for the rest of their lives. Mine happened during middle school. There I was, obliviously happy, skating through my classes and enjoying life—until a friend shared that her big brother had a crush on me. I decided that I loved him—although I'd never met him and didn't know the first thing about him, other than his jaw-dropping wonderful appearance. He and I had spoken maybe ten innocent words to each other in those first few wonderful weeks of our whirlwind romance, but I was hooked. Soon I was shocked and devastated when I saw him out with another girl. I was crushed, as were my hopes and dreams for our future together.

More heartbreak continued as I advanced in high school and college. My crushes overlooked me to date other girls—sometimes my best friends. By the time I got to college, I was approaching relationships much differently after so much disappointment. I became indifferent toward men and began to see them not as potential soulmates or future husbands, but rather just attractive props to spend an evening with at a nice restaurant to help me momentarily forget the one who'd rejected me.

If dating in college isn't confusing enough, add to that the pressure to be "good enough" to join a sorority or fraternity, and you've got a recipe for a complete identity crisis at such a young age—especially for someone who isn't secure in their identity in Christ. Satan loves to make us believe it's our own fault that we've been rejected. When I wasn't accepted into the sorority I wanted, I had thoughts like, "If only I could have gotten a couple more really good recommendations, then I'd surely have been accepted." By the time I finished college, my heart was hardened through repeated rejections. I no longer had the joyful, child-like vulnerability that I began my teenage years with.

> Above all, guard the affections of your heart, for they affect all that you are. Pay attention to the welfare of your innermost being, for from there flows the wellspring of life (Proverbs 4:23 TPT).

> I will give you a new heart and put a new spirit in you; I will remove from you your heart of stone and give you a heart of flesh (Ezekiel 36:26 NIV).

> *Dear Lord Jesus, please mend my broken heart and help me to fix my eyes on You. Help me realize that although people will disappoint and reject me, You'll always choose me and love me with an unconditional love. Please give me a new heart of flesh and help me to love others as You've loved me. In Your holy name I pray, amen.*

Numb the Pain

Do you experience feelings of hopelessness, rejection, loneliness, and despair? You're not alone. These feelings are perfectly natural in this broken world. It's okay to feel this way sometimes, and even to retreat and rest frequently in order to process trauma and loss and to heal from your wounds. However, God never intended for us to develop addictions and harmful behaviors as coping mechanisms. Instead, He invites us to rest quietly in His presence.

> And everything I've taught you is so that the peace which is in me will be in you and will give you great confidence as you rest in me. For in this unbelieving world you will experience trouble and sorrows, but you must be courageous, for I have conquered the world! (John 16:33 TPT).

Before I really knew God, I felt like an outsider in nearly every social situation. I was excluded, overlooked, quiet, and generally reserved. I thought all these were negative qualities, but the truth is that I was set apart since the time I accepted Jesus as my Lord and Savior (Deuteronomy 14:2). Because He sets us apart as His beloved, we tend to feel lonely and unloved this side of heaven. Unfortunately, I wasn't aware of this truth until I was thirty years old. As a result, college partying became my idea of fun, inclusion, and happiness.

Prior to college, I'd based my entire self-worth on my ability to give a perfect performance in school. Because I partied too much, my abilities were now failing me and I was receiving more B's and a few C's. In my mind, it wasn't just my grades that were bad—I was bad. I was no longer a perfect child, and therefore was no longer worthy of love and generosity. I didn't want to have these feelings, so I partied. The more I partied, the worse I felt. It was a vicious cycle.

My years as a young adult were not filled with light or tangible hope by any means, but God's grace was there, and I detected a bigger force at work in my life. God was a good Father even before I acknowledged Him. In His grace and mercy, He protected me from any major consequences of my new lifestyle. Late one night when I shouldn't have been driving, I went the wrong way down a one-way street. I instantly realized my mistake and was filled with dread as we approached a police officer directing traffic in an intersection. To my surprise, he used his orange light stick to kindly redirect me down the right street. What a grace-filled picture of God's love, guidance, and mercy! Even in the midst of our sin, God is always working on our behalf to rescue, direct, and restore us.

> Lord, you're so kind and tenderhearted to those who don't deserve it and so patient with people who fail you! Your love is like a flooding river overflowing its banks with kindness (Psalm 103:8 TPT).

Dear Lord Jesus, thank You for rescuing me in the midst of my sin and protecting me from serious consequences. Thank You for Your endless grace and mercy when I deserve so little from You. Please help me to show the same grace and mercy to others. In Your holy name I pray, amen.

Seeking Light in the Darkness

You may be so battered by sin and rejection that you are either waiting for death or praying for a miracle. God longs to free you from the pain and despair caused by sin. All He requires is that you ask Him. He's not going to punish or lecture you about your sin—you're already suffering the consequences in the natural realm. He wants to heal sin's ill effects in your body and mind, repair your shattered relationships, and set you on the path to glory, freedom, and prosperity.

> Surely you must know that people who practice evil cannot possess God's kingdom realm. Stop being deceived! People who continue to engage in sexual immorality, idolatry, adultery, sexual perversion, homosexuality, fraud, greed, drunkenness, verbal abuse, or extortion—these will not inherit God's kingdom realm. It's true that some of you once lived in those lifestyles, but now you have been purified from sin, made holy, and given a perfect standing before God—all because of the power of the name of the Lord Jesus, the Messiah, and through our union with the Spirit of our God (1 Corinthians 6:9-11 TPT).

As a young adult, I would try church occasionally, searching for love and acceptance. I went to a traditional Baptist church once or twice because my theology professor was the pastor and he always invited his students. Once I'd completed his course and no one was inviting me anymore, I stopped going. I had listened to the sermons, but I had not yet pursued Jesus.

I accepted an invitation to another church from a nice couple I'd met at school. Just before the Sunday morning service, I met with a small group of women from the church for Bible study. The group leader asked us to share whatever sin we were struggling with in the group. In my naivety and desire to be accepted, I shared what I thought was the worst thing about me. They all nodded in sympathetic agreement, as if they understood and had my best interest in mind.

Then we attended the main service where the pastor spoke on sin and the importance of repentance. It was good until he began lecturing specifically about the issue I'd shared earlier in the small group. It dawned on me that I'd been betrayed! I felt ashamed and completely humiliated in the middle of this congregation of strangers. I felt like they all knew my secret. I was too young to understand that I was the latest recruit in a real, live cult, but I knew something about it wasn't right and I didn't go back.

I'd tried to please some people by sharing my secrets with them, and others by partying with them. I wasn't trying to please God because I didn't know how. I continued partying and walking through the days like a zombie—utterly hopeless and alone. After one particularly bad night I felt as though I'd finally hit rock bottom. Nothing was going well, I was alone, and I felt terrible. My life was devoid of joy and the last party had not been fun. As I lay awake, intoxicated, I cried out, "God, please help me!" He had become my only option, so I simply asked Him to save me. I was hoping for a new life, much different than the one I was living.

If you're ready for a new life in Christ with all the abundance He promises to those who love Him, please say the prayer at the end of this devotional and keep it close as a reminder that He's with you and for you. Open your Bible to find out what God has to say about you, His beloved. Remember, you are His now. He has redeemed you. You are Israel, the apple of His eye.

> Protect me from harm; keep an eye on me like you would a child reflected in the twinkling of your eye. Yes,

hide me within the shelter of your embrace, under your outstretched wings (Psalm 17:8 TPT).

Dear Lord Jesus, thank You for Your sacrifice, kindness, forgiveness, and grace. I'm sorry for my lifestyle. I've made mistakes, and I'm ready to live for You. Please forgive me, heal me, and show me how to live. You're my Lord and Savior, and I can do nothing apart from You. Please give me hope, peace, joy, blessing, protection, provision, favor, and love. In Your holy name I pray, amen.

Finding Love

An answered prayer can feel like a giant hug and a jackpot win, all in one. Stories abound of God's rapid response time and miraculous healing power when a distraught parent cries out to Him to save their child from illness or injury. These are life-or-death situations which require an immediate response. However, don't be discouraged if you're praying for blessings, love, or guidance, and His miracle is delayed. Know that while you're waiting on an answer to your prayer, God is preparing you to receive it.

> I was desperate for you to help me in my struggles, and
> you did! (Psalm 120:1 TPT).

Not long after the pivotal incident in my college apartment bedroom when I cried out to the Lord for help, He introduced me to my wonderful husband, Nick. I arrived at his house one day with my Latin books and some notes with the intention of helping my classmate (also Nick's roommate) study for our upcoming exam. Although my classmate may have intended to ask me out, it was Nick I liked and eventually went on a date with.

When we were dating, Nick was always a gentleman, ever ready to whisk me off to our next exciting adventure. We had so much fun whenever we were together, and he always went the extra mile to make me feel loved, special, and protected. I continued to party, but I felt much safer with him. Once when my feet were hurting in the cheap, too-small cowboy boots I'd worn to a concert, he carried me on his back as he walked the two or three miles home. We each made sure that the other had a relatively safe ride home after a night out. We'd recover the next day with coffee and painful exercise sessions at the park or gym. He took me on dates frequently and taxied me to and from my classes.

In spite of our blossoming romance, a dark cloud followed me around and put an emotional damper on much of our time together. Our happiest, most hope-filled times were often overshadowed by ghosts of our pasts. We'd both been rejected by lesser loves and social clubs, and hurt by religion—and these frustrations often bubbled to the surface. The devil masterfully wields cycles of bondage to keep us in constant turmoil. If we're not focused on Jesus, past hurts can linger, affecting our behavior so we continue injuring ourselves and wounding others in our wake. I'd say hurtful things when I was tired and then feel like a failure. There were a few mornings when I woke up and wondered if I'd ever see Nick again, but, miraculously, he forgave me every time.

Fortunately, Nick loved me enough to walk beside me through every mistake and misunderstanding. It wasn't long after we began dating when he gently whispered to me that he loved me, and I told him that I loved him too. That Christmas he bought me a beautiful diamond and platinum ring. Maybe he knew from the beginning he would be in it for the long haul, no matter what. He didn't run from my problems. He helped me carry them, just as Jesus modeled for us all.

> *Love empowers us to* fulfill the law of the Anointed One as we carry each other's troubles (Galatians 6:2 TPT).

> *Dear Lord Jesus, I'm in such desperate need of (put your own needs here). You've seen my struggles, so please hear my prayer. I also need help forgiving (put the names of people you'd like to forgive) so that I can move on into the plans You have for me. Please heal me so I can help others instead of hurting them. In Your holy name I pray, amen.*

Marriage

The story of Hosea and Gomer seems to represent God's redeeming love for us, His bride (Isaiah 54:5). God instructed the prophet Hosea to take an unlikely bride. Hosea cares for, pursues, and redeems his rebellious wife. She's a runaway bride who is controlled by her emotions and continually drawn back to her former life. In obedience to God's command that he love her unconditionally, Hosea purchases his wife out of the slavery she left him for.

This is the same unconditional love that led God to accept death on the cross as redemptive payment for the sins of mankind. As a result, you are forever justified in your Father's eyes. He pursues each of us in our sin and speaks tenderly to us in the wilderness we inevitably find ourselves in. It is His kindness that draws us back to Him and all the good things He has planned for us, including prosperity, freedom, hope, and a future as His heirs (Jeremiah 29:11).

God loves marriage and hates divorce. When two married people are devoted to God first then to each other and their children, they are a force to be reckoned with for His kingdom as sons and daughters of the Most High King. It's this holy anointing and confidence that allows couples to advance God's kingdom by fighting poverty, spreading the gospel, and carrying His healing presence to the weak and broken. Jesus explained it to the Pharisees this way:

> From the beginning God created male and female. For this reason a man will leave his parents and be wedded to his wife. And the husband and wife will be joined as one flesh, and after that they no longer exist as two, but one flesh. So there you have it. What God has joined together, no one has the right to split apart (Mark 10:6-9 TPT).

Nick proposed to me in 2004 as we were just out of college, and we married a year later. Throughout our marriage, I have seen God's love in Nick. Like the lamb in Nathan's prophecy to David, I have shared his food, drank from his cup, and slept in his arms (2 Samuel 12:3). We've both sacrificed out of love for each other, relinquishing some old dreams for new ones we will build together.

> To the fatherless he is a father. To the widow he is a champion friend. To the lonely he makes them part of a family. To the prisoners he leads into prosperity until they sing for joy. This is our Holy God in his Holy Place! (Psalm 68:5-6 TPT).

> *Dear Lord Jesus, thank You for the wonderful gift of marriage. Please let mine be a beautiful picture of Your love for everyone. Help me always speak kindly to my family. Let my kids desire the kind of marriage You've given us. Please strengthen us so we can be a force for love in Your kingdom. In Your holy name I pray, amen.*

Firstborn

God gives us countless and varied opportunities for success and promotion in life. You may fail a test every now and then, but, just like a perfect father would, He is faithful to let you take it again and again until you succeed. If you have children, you experience rebirth and renewal in childbirth. In giving life, we are born again as parents.

Eve was the first woman redeemed through childbirth. Later on in Scripture, Hosea saved Gomer, and her redemption culminated in motherhood. God's love spared their lives, but their children justified these women before men and filled their lives with new joy and purpose. They were given a second chance at a fulfilling life through motherhood.

> Yet a woman shall live in restored dignity by means of
> her children, receiving the blessing that comes from
> raising them as consecrated children nurtured in faith
> and love, walking in wisdom (1 Timothy 2:15 TPT).

Nick and I were blessed with our first child, Jackson, the morning of December 27, 2011. This was the very day my obstetrician predicted he would arrive. He was born healthy and now he's smart, funny, sweet, spunky, and precious. Children make everything so joyous! When Jackson was just learning to speak, my heart melted every time he said he loved me or when I'd hear him ask his Dad about me.

Parenting well means protecting, and protecting often involves discipline. Once I dreamed that Jackson tiptoed around the head of a sleeping bear without waking it. I interpreted this to mean that the Lord will always protect him, which I've witnessed. This is true of all of my children. I still worry when they attempt to stick things in electrical outlets or dart off the sidewalk and into the street. My reaction to stop them and sternly explain the danger isn't to cruelly deprive them of all they want to do, but rather to save their lives.

Although I can be quick to judge when it appears that other parents haven't adequately disciplined their kids (albeit less so, now that I have four), I usually have the opposite response to God's discipline of me. I think, "Why is He letting this happen to me?" But the trials we endure are part of His loving plan for our correction and restoration. We must not blame Him when bad things happen, because He does not cause them. Fortunately, God allows us to feel the pain from sin so we will realize that it is harmful and repent, turning toward Him to seek healing.

> And have you forgotten his encouraging words spoken to you as his children? He said, "My child, don't underestimate the value of the discipline and training of the Lord God, or get depressed when he has to correct you. For the Lord's training of your life is the evidence of his faithful love. And when he draws you to himself, it proves you are his delightful child" (Hebrews 12:5-6 TPT).

Dear Lord Jesus, thank You for the gifts of sonship, training, free will, and pain receptors. To be fully Yours, I understand that You'll correct me from time to time for my own benefit. Help me to discern and appreciate Your discipline. In Your holy name I pray, amen.

New Friend

I began to understand how Jesus feels about His children after I had children of my own. My love for my kids is a mere reflection of the Father's love for me; His love is perfect, while human love can falter when situations spin out of control or moods take over. The Lord loves us unconditionally, which helps explain what He endured on the cross in order to reconcile us to Himself. He never intended for us to live in isolation, apart from Him or other people.

> Two people are better off than one, for they can help each other succeed. If one person falls, the other can reach out and help. But someone who falls alone is in real trouble. Likewise, two people lying close together can keep each other warm. But how can one be warm alone? A person standing alone can be attacked and defeated, but two can stand back-to-back and conquer (Ecclesiastes 4:9-12 NLT).

I prayed for a sibling for Jackson for months during a time of deep sadness and emotional suffering. I knew a new baby would bring healing and hope to our family and so, like Hannah, I prayed. I knew Jackson and his new sibling would become best friends—and they have. I remember the fun texts my husband and I exchanged the day I told him the big news about Charlie. We were going to be a family of four! I'd been an only child who wished for siblings, so I knew every child needs a lifelong friend they've played with ever since they could remember.

My second pregnancy was difficult due to severe nausea and a couple of really rough bouts with a stomach virus. I was amazed I could endure such illness and suffering while carrying a perfectly-healthy baby. God's divine protection must extend into the womb to cover His innocents. I awoke about four a.m. on May 17, 2015, to mildly painful contractions and knew it was time to head to the hospital.

Charles was born in an inflated birthing tub full of warm water. I leaned on the Lord that happy day to help me through several hours of excruciating labor pains. We listened to worship music, and between each contraction I said the Lord's Prayer over and over until, at last, Charlie emerged from my body into the water! I felt great after the unmedicated delivery and was able to hop in and out of bed afterward to greet the many visitors we had.

We named our second child Charles after my Dad, and Edward (his middle name) after Nick's Dad, but Charlie looks exactly like his own dad. He's got big, beautiful brown eyes that make him appear vulnerable and innocent (which he is), although he is also the warrior that the name "Charles" signifies. He looks like a cherub angel from a classical painting.

A prophetic Christian artist created a painting of Charlie and Jackson from a photograph I gave her. She first met Charlie in our home one day just after his nap and immediately said to him, "You're a warrior!" I already knew that's what his name meant, but she didn't. The Lord had just revealed Charlie's identity to her. The painting she completed several weeks later depicts the boys walking along a stream (of living water) through the woods, followed closely by a warrior angel wielding a fiery sword. True to the painting, our children walk closely with the Lord under the protection of His hosts.

> God sends angels with special orders to protect you
> wherever you go, defending you from all harm
> (Psalm 91:11 TPT).

Dear Lord Jesus, thank You for Your sacrifice, for giving me access to you, and for becoming my friend (John 15:15). Please help me to be a good friend and help me make new ones. In Your holy name I pray, amen.

Full Quiver

Our Lord longs to give you the desires of your heart, even though you may not yet be able to identify what those are. Don't worry; He'll guide your prayers and show you just what to ask for. He sees well into our future and knows what will bring us the most joy, and often delivers those things to us without even being asked! He understands everything about you, knowing even better than you what (or who) can fill the deep voids in your heart.

> Children are God's love-gift; they are heaven's generous reward. Children born to a young couple will one day rise to protect and provide for their parents. Happy will be the couple who has many of them! A household full of children will not bring shame on your name but victory when you face your enemies, for your offspring will have influence and honor to prevail on your behalf! (Psalm 127:3-5 TPT).

In February 2016, Nick and I were invited to a fundraising gala through a handwritten invitation from the director of a huge, wonderful, faith-based, charitable organization located just outside southwest Atlanta: the Midwest Food Bank. The evening was incredibly special, considering all the event details: its location at Pinewood Studios, my beautiful white dress, and my handsome date. My mother took photos of us just before the gala.

For months prior, I'd had a recurring dream of preparing for a wedding of my own, including the selection of a white dress. I failed to connect the dream with the upcoming gala until a few days before the event when I received a white dress I'd ordered online. It fit perfectly the first time I put it on. I believe the Lord had given me the dreams as a foreshadowing of this event as a second wedding, with my mom as a special attendant.

Evelyn arrived nine months later, on November 23, 2016, in a birthing tub in our house. When our brand new, perfectly healthy and beautiful, answer-to-prayer baby girl was just five months old and sleeping peacefully in her crib, we experienced a catastrophic April downpour. As it rained, water leaked into our house and a portion of the drywall ceiling in Evy's room became so heavy with rainwater that it broke away and fell to the floor. Huge chunks landed in the crib where she slept. I did not think she had survived.

Miraculously, under all the debris we found a very frightened but perfectly safe baby. The chunks of ceiling appeared to have landed around her at angles (with the help of angels) so that she was untouched beneath. She didn't have a scratch, just some dust in her hair, and she was smiling soon afterward. We praised the Lord as we celebrated her miraculous survival!

Our fourth baby and third little boy, Nicholas Jr., was born in April of 2018. This was a difficult labor. I fainted in my bathroom shortly after my water broke, just after a too-hot shower as I was sitting on the porcelain throne. I came to on my knees and forearms, belly safe. Because of the way I'd landed, neither of us were hurt. Only God could do that! Further, baby Nick's umbilical cord was wrapped around his neck twice. As a result, labor didn't progress quickly. He was finally born, healthy and happy, just outside the tub on a pile of towels next to an exhausted mama. By the time he was three months old, we decided to sell what was beginning to feel like a tiny three-bedroom house and upgrade to something a bit roomier. Baby Nick's arrival had officially made us a big family!

> I look up to the mountains and hills, longing for God's help. But then I realize that our true help and protection come only from the Lord, our Creator who made the heavens and the earth. He will guard and guide me, never letting me stumble or fall. God is my keeper; he

will never forget nor ignore me. He will never slumber nor sleep; he is the Guardian-God for his people, Israel. Jehovah himself will watch over you; he's always at your side to shelter you safely in his presence. He's protecting you from all danger both day and night. He will keep you from every form of evil or calamity as he continually watches over you. You will be guarded by God himself. You will be safe when you leave your home and safely you will return. He will protect you now, and he'll protect you forevermore! (Psalm 121 TPT).

Dear Lord Jesus, thank You for Your many beautiful blessings and for Your constant protection. Please keep me and my family safe and healthy, healing all our illnesses and thwarting the enemy's plans against us. Please give us the opportunity to protect and bless others as You've done for us. In Your holy name I pray, amen.

Exposure

God warns us to be spiritually vigilant, but also assures us that we have His help and love, especially through our mistakes and the enemy's attacks. He wants you to know He is real and cares for you, so He may reveal Himself by manifesting physically, allowing you to sense His nearness. He may also draw your attention to the devil's schemes to steal, kill, and destroy. Once these plans are exposed and made obvious, the Lord can guide you out of harm's way.

> Be alert and of sober mind. Your enemy the devil prowls
> around like a roaring lion looking for someone to devour.
> (1 Peter 5:8 NIV).

I remember listening to a song in late 2013 that I now understand to be heretical, or at odds with God's will and Word. It's not obviously offensive without paying close attention to the lyrics. It presumes to tell the story of Jesus' life, and does so mostly in a respectful manner until it addresses the crucifixion. The subtle, yet twisted suggestion is that while Jesus hung on the cross, He blamed Himself for the wretched state of the world. The truth is that man freely chose a sinful nature in Eden.

I liked the song then, so I added it to my public playlist. Without missing a beat, five dead leaves simultaneously fell from different stalks on the tall "money tree" (cute houseplant with a braided trunk) that sat on our desk, all landing in a pile in front of me. With the fallen leaves, God had my attention—but I stubbornly chose to run out for a quick errand instead of heeding His urge to address the issue immediately.

I hopped in my car and was pulling out of the driveway when I stopped to admire a woodpecker, adorned with a bright red cap and hopping up the trunk of the biggest tree in our yard. I had never seen one so close. I knew God had His hand in this too. Later, as I searched online for meaning in what I had seen, I discovered that woodpeckers, due to their destructive nature, are typically associated with the enemy.

The enemy comes only to steal, kill, and destroy, although through deception he can initially appear attractive and can gain entry into our lives through invitation. That day I realized that I had to be very careful about what I invited into my home and exposed myself and my family to. Dead music and heretical messages are dangerous. Most online interactions also provide the opportunity to influence those who follow us, so we should consider the messages we send with our clicks. Now I try not to listen to music with any messages which are contrary to God's Word.

> So keep your thoughts continually fixed on all that is authentic and real, honorable and admirable, beautiful and respectful, pure and holy, merciful and kind. (Philippians 4:8 TPT).

> *Dear Lord Jesus, please shield me and my family from harmful and dangerous influence. Protect our minds and hearts so we can shine brightly for You. Please give us discernment and warnings to steer us away from destruction and toward Your protective, loving embrace. In Your holy name I pray, amen.*

Fiery Trials

The trials that draw us nearest to God are often the ones we experience by ourselves—only with Him. Sometimes no one else can understand what we're going through because of their limited perspective. It may be difficult to find joy in the specific events and details of each trial because they are painful. It is instead the whole experience of the trial that produces a stronger faith, resulting in joy every time.

> My fellow believers, when it seems as though you are facing
> nothing but difficulties see it as an invaluable opportunity
> to experience the greatest joy that you can! For you know
> that when your faith is tested it stirs up power within you
> to endure all things (James 1:2-3 TPT).

I don't believe anyone can be prepared for the trials of pregnancy, delivery, and having a newborn. Pre-natal nausea alone is enough to shake anyone's faith. Being pregnant, tired, and sick is an incredibly lonely time. Nothing seems fun—and the smallest tasks seem nearly impossible. I spent as much time as possible sleeping and eating, because those were the only times when the nausea, depression, and exhaustion subsided.

I'd been terrified of gaining weight since I was in middle school. So gaining fifty-plus pounds while pregnant with Jackson in 2011 had a very negative effect on my self-image. I resolved to lose the weight quickly after Jackson was born. In fact, I was doing yoga the day after giving birth. A week after giving birth, I was jogging. Although I was not an extreme exerciser, I was devoted to my relatively-short daily workout.

I shed weight rapidly until one day when I stepped on the scale and weighed in at less than one hundred pounds. In the two years since giving birth, I'd lost more than seventy pounds. I was trying on the smallest sized clothes, only to discover that they were too big for me. I could see the bones under the skin on my chest and I was afraid. For the first time in a long time—maybe ever—I worried that I didn't weigh enough.

Yoga is intimately connected with demon worship and the poses are prayer positions to those spirits, opening the practitioner up to spiritual influence. Although I never formally or deliberately embraced the religious aspect of yoga, I was still influenced negatively. I had assumed that I could perform the poses innocuously, purely for exercise. When I stopped practicing, I began hearing unwanted voices/sounds when trying to sleep, sounds that no one else could hear. I believe these disturbances were demonic harassment, but God allowed it for a time because He wanted me awake to the destructive nature of my behavior. After several years of stubborn refusal to acknowledge that yoga is a dangerous spiritual practice, I finally understood. I found and prayed a prayer of renouncement to break off any ties or agreements with the enemy that may have been formed through the practice.

I have found that God often confirms His messages for us multiple times for emphasis and urgency, and He did this for me during this life-or-death situation. He may use worldly objects that symbolize something else, I think, to encourage us to do some research and discover the hidden meanings. Several days after I weighed in at less than one hundred pounds, Jackson began saying to me, "cuckoo, bye-bye, cuckoo, bye-bye." I looked up the Christian meaning of the cuckoo bird, and it means, "lean, thin."[1] God used Jackson to confirm that I was going bye-bye if I didn't stop binge exercising!

1. "Bible Animals: Cuckoo," Bible History Online, accessed December 12, 2019, https://www.bible-history.com/links.php?cat=41&sub=842&cat_name=Bible+Animals&subcat_name=Cuckoo.

I stopped exercising, but it seemed I could not stop losing weight. I even began to find it difficult to eat, although I desperately needed to. I could eat only a few bites before I felt full, but that was not enough to keep up with the rate at which I burned calories. Breastfeeding requires extra calories, and yoga is effective at toning the body so that it becomes very lean. The resulting muscle tissue burns more calories than body fat, even while the body is at rest. One day I read Psalm 107:18-21 (ESV) which says, "They loathed any kind of food, and drew near the gates of death. Then they cried out to the Lord in their trouble, and He delivered them from their destruction. Let them thank the Lord for His steadfast love, for His wondrous works to the children of man!" I knew at that moment that with God's help, I would soon be able to eat, increase my body fat (update: success!), and normalize my metabolism.

My intake had to outpace my metabolism if I were to recover. I purposely ate more than I felt was enough, didn't exercise, and began to gain some weight. After a couple of weeks of intentional weight gain, I began to feel stronger and could enjoy food again. I had so much more energy to play with Jackson without becoming exhausted each day. God was also preparing me to have more children. Gradually I was able to eat normally without the fear of gaining weight, and Charlie was born in the spring of 2015.

Today I feel good, am a bit heavier, and try not to worry about my weight and appearance. I haven't started back on an exercise routine yet, other than keeping up with my four little ones—which is probably plenty for the moment! I thank God for His divine intervention, especially in times of imminent danger, and for His good and perfect gifts from above. I'm also learning to love and accept myself, no matter what the scale says.

> For athletic training only benefits you for a short season,
> but righteousness brings lasting benefit in everything;
> for righteousness contains the promise of life, for time
> and eternity (1 Timothy 4:8 TPT).

Dear Lord Jesus, thank You for waking me up to my destructive habits before it's too late. Help me to pursue You and the things that please You first, understanding that as long as I'm healthy, it doesn't really matter what I look like. In Your holy name I pray, amen.

Free and Cleansed

You must remember how quickly the Lord forgives you when you fall. His punishment on the cross compensates for your faults, so you are instantly and forever justified before God once you accept Him as Lord and Savior and ask for His forgiveness. Repent of your sins often for your own sake. God knows your faults and has forgiven you even before you make a mistake, so live to please God rather than man (the latter is nearly impossible, particularly without God's grace and favor). Live for God; for if He is with you, who can be against you? (See Romans 8:31.)

> Be imitators of God in everything you do, for then you will represent your Father as his beloved sons and daughters. And continue to walk surrendered to the extravagant love of Christ, for he surrendered his life as a sacrifice for us. His great love for us was pleasing to God, like an aroma of adoration—a sweet healing fragrance (Ephesians 5:1-2 TPT).

As I mentioned in the previous story, along with my freedom from the bondage of over-exercise came demonic harassment and sleeplessness. Satan doesn't give up easily. I was free and cleansed by the blood of Jesus—and satan was mad! Bedtime had become a bit scary and confusing for me. I didn't know what types of noises I was going to hear or how long they would keep me up, so I adopted the phrase "I trust you, Jesus" as my only sleep aid. I said it silently each night until I drifted off to sleep, learning to place all my trust in the Lord.

One morning during this same time, I realized that I couldn't find my wedding ring set. Looking all over the house would be futile, as it could be anywhere. Much like facing the monsters at bedtime each night, waiting for the lost ring would also be an exercise of trust in God. I trusted Him to put it in my path to find and, as He often does with seemingly ordinary incidents, to show me something deeper. I remembered Psalm 46:10 (NLT) which says, "Be still, and know that I am God." In other words, calm down and let God handle the situations we can't control. That afternoon I was pulling wet clothes out of the washing machine and heard a "clink" as the ring bounced out of the machine and onto the floor beside me. It was clean, shiny, and looked brand new. The symbolism of finding my ring with His help was instantly obvious: God was newly blessing my marriage of nearly nine years through renewal and forgiveness, which are likely similar to the blessings of a formal vow renewal.

> Yahweh, you are my soul's celebration. How could I ever forget the miracles of kindness you've done for me? You kissed my heart with forgiveness, in spite of all I've done. You've healed me inside and out from every disease. You've rescued me from hell and saved my life. You've crowned me with love and mercy (Psalm 103:2-4 TPT).

> *Dear Lord Jesus, thank You for Your endless fount of mercy and forgiveness, and for showing me how to trust You when things seem really scary and hopeless. Thank You for finding, cleansing, and protecting me, Your lost sheep. In Your holy name I pray, amen.*

I Am

Scripture describes the varied nature of God as He relates to you, His beloved. God is your protective shepherd (John 10), a place you can rest, gentle and humble (Matthew 11:28-30), patient and merciful (Psalm 145:8), our Savior, our King, our God. He is everything to you, and He is always with you (Matthew 1:23). God is just what you need in every situation, wherever you are in life, whether you've just discovered Him or have known His love for a long time.

> Are you weary, carrying a heavy burden? Then come to me. I will refresh your life, for I am your oasis. Simply join your life with mine. Learn my ways and you'll discover that I'm gentle, humble, easy to please. You will find refreshment and rest in me (Matthew 11:28-29 TPT).

When God spoke quietly to me one lonely college night in Athens, Georgia, I probably didn't hear Him. I cried out to Him in the dark from my apartment bedroom, and I'm sure He answered, "I am here, and you are Mine." I didn't hear Him that night—or any time at all—until about ten years later when He literally spoke to me in the bedroom of the house I was living in with my husband and son.

A thunderstorm woke me the morning of April 29, 2014. At the first two rumbles of thunder, I heard "I Am" spoken each time. The words were audible only to me, I heard them clearly in my spirit. I felt peace, knowing it was an assurance from our Lord Jesus. I'd not slept well for several months, but that morning I woke well-rested and happy to hear from Him.

Jesus uses the words "I Am" throughout the book of John to identify himself as the Bread of Life, the Light of the World, the Door, the True

Vine, the Good Shepherd, the Resurrection and the Life, and the Way, the Truth, and the Life. In the Old Testament, God instructed Moses to tell the Egyptians that he was sent by "I Am" (Exodus 3:14). The Prophet Isaiah spoke this message to Israel from God:

> Do not yield to fear, for I am always near. Never turn your gaze from me, for I am your faithful God. I will infuse you with my strength and help you in every situation. I will hold you firmly with my victorious right hand (Isaiah 41:10 TPT).

Dear Lord Jesus, thank You for revealing Yourself and Your loving nature to me. Thank You for being so many wonderful things to me and always making sure I have what I need. Please continue to help me understand You and Your ways through dreams, visions, miracles, and prophecies. In Your holy name I pray, amen.

Mysteries Unveiled

I f you look up at the sky on a clear night, it is impossible not to feel like you're communing with God. He invites you to turn toward and look upon Him from wherever you are, and to be saved (Isaiah 45:22). Where can anyone on Planet Earth look and have the same view as someone on the other side of the world? Only to the sky, of course! You and I have a front-row seat to God's heavenly light show. The sky is beautiful to behold, but the heavens also announce His plans and purposes to the entire world.

> And God said, "Let there be lights in the vault of the sky to separate the day from the night, and let them serve as signs to mark sacred times, and days and years" (Genesis 1:14 NIV).

The Lord has countless ways to commune with us. One night in early 2014, just before falling asleep I received an audible message from the Lord. He said, "The sun will be darkened." The message was clear, concise, and truthful. It was only audible to me, and it sounded to me much like Scripture. I found the exact statement in the verses from Matthew 24, noted below. He spoke to me so that I would seek to learn more about Him, which I did.

Two weeks later I was in the audience at ABBA's House in Chattanooga, listening to Pastor John Hagee speak about his book *Four Blood Moons*. He was explaining the timeline for the upcoming total lunar eclipses and associated global events. He referenced several instances in the Bible which describe visible astronomical events, including Matthew 24:29. As he spoke, that verse with the very words I'd heard from the Lord two weeks prior was projected on the big screens.

Four total lunar eclipses (or blood moons) occurred in 2014 and 2015, and a solar eclipse (a darkened sun) occurred in March of 2015, the month following Pastor Hagee's sermon. Just as God foretells global events with public messages in the sky, He also foretold with a personal message that I would be at ABBA's House. This encouraged me to study what Scripture has to say about end times and how He uses the celestial bodies to communicate with us. It also prepared me for the day I'd literally see His face in the clouds.

> Then immediately this is what will take place: "The sun will be darkened and the moon give no light. The stars will fall from the sky and all the cosmic powers will be shaken." Then the sign announcing the Son of Man will appear in the sky, and all the nations of the earth will mourn over him. And they will see the Son of Man appearing in the clouds of heaven, revealed with mighty power, great splendor, and glory (Matthew 24:29-30 TPT).

> *Dear Lord Jesus, thank You for taking such great care to communicate with Your beloved through all of our senses. Help us remember to look up, behold Your beautiful creation, and ask You what You're trying to tell the world. In Your holy name I pray, amen.*

His Face

Have you said or done something that you regret so much that you were afraid life might not go on in the wake of your mistake? Maybe your reaction to someone else's words or actions seems unforgivable. Please understand that God sees the purity of your heart and does not intend to punish you. Instead, He's going to heal your mistakes and wounds and knit the broken pieces back together as only He can.

> *I pray with great faith for you*, because I'm fully convinced that the One who began this glorious work in you will faithfully continue the process of maturing you and will put his finishing touches to it until the unveiling of our Lord Jesus Christ! (Philippians 1:6 TPT).

One evening during a family vacation, Nick and I began arguing immediately after dinner. During the five minutes it took to walk back to the hotel room we'd said some really hurtful things to each other. In those dark moments when every second seems uncertain and death appears to be knocking at the door, escape through substance abuse is an attractive solution. But escape doesn't pair well with young children. Too many times children pay the price for their parents' mistakes. I thank God for my resolve in that particular situation to "stay calm and carry on," as if adhering to our nighttime routine would act like glue and hold life together.

Miraculously, Nick and I reconciled first thing in the morning. We realized we'd both been wrong and didn't want to ruin our exciting plans for the day. (Our reconciliation is further detailed in the Part III story, *His Favor Lasts a Lifetime*) Back at home, I sat by myself in the living room feeling peaceful and relieved. As I gazed out the window at the gray summertime clouds I saw HIS face—God's majestic, chiseled, bearded, white profile was clearly on display in the clouds. I was looking at my Creator! His appearance was perfectly consistent with Scripture: "His head and his hair were white like wool—white as glistening snow" (Revelation 1:14 TPT). I marveled at Him for a few long, luxurious seconds until, in vain, I left the window to get my phone for a photograph.

In those moments, I suddenly understood God's love for me. He instantly destroyed all the enemy's lies I'd ever believed about myself. I wasn't a bad person, a bad mom, a bad wife or daughter. I wasn't at fault, I wasn't to blame, and I certainly wasn't supposed to feel any more guilt or shame for anything in my past. I'm the beloved daughter of the Most High King, righteous and pure in heart because of His ultimate sacrifice! It wasn't long after this miracle when I came across Matthew 5:8 (NIV): Blessed are the pure in heart, for they will see God.

> We look away from the natural realm and we fasten our gaze onto Jesus who birthed faith within us and who leads us forward into faith's perfection. His example is this: Because his heart was focused on the joy of knowing that you would be his, he endured the agony of the cross and conquered its humiliation, and now sits exalted at the right hand of the throne of God! (Hebrews 12:2 TPT).

> And at last, when you see how the Son of Man comes— surrounded with a cloud, with great power and miracles, in the radiance of his splendor, and with great glory and praises—it will make you jump for joy! For the day of your full transformation has arrived (Luke 21:27-28 TPT).

> *Dear Lord Jesus, thank You for all the careful and thoughtful ways you reveal Yourself to me. Thank You for helping me understand how You see me through Your lens of unconditional love. Thank You for piecing together all of my shattered pieces. Help me to see myself and others as You see us. In your holy name I pray, amen.*

Part 2:

Deliverance

Let me be clear, the Anointed One has set us free—not partially, but completely and wonderfully free!

Galatians 5:1 (TPT)

Trapped

Have you ever felt trapped in your circumstances—alone in the dark with no one who cares or wants to help? Don't worry about how you got there, even if you blame yourself. Although we may impose darkness and danger on ourselves, God's light will find us, lifting us out of the dark and back on our feet. He sees you in the dark and will come to your rescue if you'll just ask. He waits to be invited into our messes.

> I waited and waited and waited some more, patiently, knowing God would come through for me. Then, at last, he bent down and listened to my cry. He stooped down to lift me out of danger from the desolate pit I was in, out of the muddy mess I had fallen into. Now he's lifted me up into a firm, secure place and steadied me while I walk along his ascending path. A new song for a new day rises up in me every time I think about how he breaks through for me! Ecstatic praise pours out of my mouth until everyone hears how God has set me free. Many will see his miracles; they'll stand in awe of God and fall in love with him! (Psalm 40:1-3 TPT).

It was pitch black, silent, and oppressively hot. I tried desperately to push the seat forward to exit the same way I had just entered, but it had locked into place and I was trapped. I had played in the car many times before, crawling in and out of the trunk through the back seat. It folded down to allow trunk access, but this time it wouldn't open. As the heat began to build, I panicked and screamed. I screamed as loud as I could for several minutes. It is impossible to explain how alone, afraid, and helpless I felt as a little girl trapped inside the trunk of my Mom's sedan on a hot Georgia summer day.

Dad was at work and Mom, who was a teacher and had summers off, was inside the house. There was no way she could hear me screaming, but I kept screaming because it was my only option. But the more I screamed, the hotter it got inside the trunk—and the harder it was for me to breathe. I don't know how long I was trapped, but it couldn't have been too long in those conditions. It probably felt much longer than it actually was.

After several terrifying minutes, the trunk door suddenly popped open, sunlight streamed in, and fresh air filled my lungs. Even the hot, humid air felt cool and welcome against my skin. My mom had heard me; although I remember her saying that she wasn't sure how she possibly could have. Not only had she heard my screams that were insulated in the car parked in the driveway, away from the house, but she'd also heard them over loud music playing inside the house. It must have been by divine grace and power—not by her own ability.

> The splendor light of heaven's glorious sunrise is about to break upon us in holy visitation, all because the merciful heart of our God is so very tender (Luke 1:78 TPT).

> *Dear Lord Jesus, thank You for rescuing me. Sometimes I feel very alone and afraid, wondering if it's the end for me. Thank You for always hearing my cries and sending Your angels. Please give me the opportunity to help rescue others as You've done for me. In Your holy name I pray, amen.*

Drowning

Have you ever found yourself in a situation you thought you could handle, only to soon realize that you were in over your head, struggling to catch your breath? Perhaps you've overcommitted and it's too late to back out of the projects. Maybe your temptations have drawn you into the deep and you've begun to sink into the darkness. I have good news! With Jesus, it's never too late for rescue and restoration. He hears your cries.

> Lord, I cry out to you out of the depths of my despair!
> Hear my voice, O God! Answer this prayer and hear my
> plea for mercy…O Israel, keep hoping, keep trusting, and
> keep waiting on the Lord, for he is tenderhearted, kind,
> and forgiving. He has a thousand ways to set you free!
> He himself will redeem you; he will ransom you from
> the cruel slavery of your sins! (Psalm 130:1-2, 7-8 TPT).

Long ago, before we had kids, Nick and I were vacationing at a beach along the Gulf of Mexico. On one particular day, the beach was crowded and people were in the ocean despite the red flags warning about dangerous undertow conditions. The atmosphere was strange, with many people in the water in imminent danger. Some were aware of it as they struggled against the undercurrents, while some swam obliviously happy in calmer water. Most people on the beach played and lounged, while others began to take notice and call people to come out of the water.

Nick and I joined the rebellious bunch of swimmers that day. We ignored the warning flags and had waded out a good distance from the shore when suddenly the undertow lifted us both off our feet, separated us, and carried us farther away from shore. I didn't know that an undertow is easy to escape if you remain calm and swim parallel to the shore. Unfortunately, my first reactions were panic and resistance, trying to swim against the current back to safety, and becoming quickly exhausted. My head went below water several times, which only added to my terror and feelings of helplessness. In my panic, I ignored God's presence and forgot His power.

Nick had the strength to swim and began to make progress toward the beach, while I floundered. He was too far away to reach, so I called out desperately, hoping he would rescue me. I was losing hope, felt terrified, and was saddened by my situation. I felt remorse for not heeding the warnings and respecting what had already happened to other unfortunate swimmers that week. News reports said that at least six people had drowned in the area that week because of the strong undertow, and dozens of others had been carried away from shore by it. I was about to join them.

Although it seemed like a long time, I think I struggled only a matter of minutes before a strong wave came along and lifted me above the power of the current. It carried me a long way quickly, depositing me near a family standing in shallow water. One of them grabbed my hand so I wouldn't be washed away again before I could stand up. Nick was right behind me. God had pulled us both from the water.

After a brief rest in the sand, we approached the water to see how many were still swimming and how they were faring. I spotted a tiny person bobbing about the same distance from shore as we had been when swept away. Nick determined that she needed help, although it wasn't immediately apparent to anyone else. Though exhausted, he grabbed a random boogie board and headed back into the ocean he had just escaped from. He'd barely reached her when a few other men spotted them and decided to assist with the rescue effort. All five made it back safe and sound. We were all grateful for Nick's bravery and God's faithfulness.

> But when he realized how high the waves were, he (Peter) became frightened and started to sink. "Save me,

Lord!" he cried out. Jesus immediately stretched out his hand and lifted him up and said, "What little faith you have! Why would you let doubt win?" And the very moment they both stepped into the boat, the raging wind ceased. Then all the disciples crouched down before him and worshiped Jesus. They said in adoration, "You are truly the Son of God!" (Matthew 14:30-33 TPT).

Dear Lord Jesus, thank You for Your faithfulness in life-or-death situations. I know You're always ready with a strong arm to lift me above the waves. Please give me more opportunities to help those struggling and in danger, especially those who are weak and defenseless. In Your holy name I pray, amen.

Nightmare

Not only will God rescue your physical body, He will also send His angels to deliver your mind from peril. Satan would like to see all of us trapped—living as prisoners to lies, regrets, fear, and confusion. God will heal your mind from whatever you're struggling with; from depression, anxiety, and sleeplessness, to chronic disorders like autism, dementia, and schizophrenia. It's His will that your mind be restored to clarity, peace, and rest.

> The Lord is my best friend and my shepherd. I always have more than enough. He offers a resting place for me in his luxurious love. His tracks take me to an oasis of peace, the quiet brook of bliss…Lord, even when your path takes me through the valley of deepest darkness, fear will never conquer me, for you already have! You remain close to me and lead me through it all the way. Your authority is my strength and my peace. The comfort of your love takes away my fear. I'll never be lonely, for you are near (Psalm 23:1-2, 4 TPT).

One afternoon when Jackson, my firstborn, was two, I retired to my room for a nap after he went to sleep in his room. I was awakened by music, specifically an instrumental version of *Hark the Herald Angels*. I knew it must be coming from a children's book of the same title given to Jackson by my aunt when he was born. The book plays the song when the star-shaped button on the front cover is pushed. At this particular time, the book was lying on the nightstand beside my bed when it played the tune. No one but me had been in the room to push the button.

At the same time, I realized that I'd started to have a very bad dream when the book woke me, so I was grateful. In my dream, a heavy metal rock song had begun to play and unpleasant scenery was beginning to manifest. After I'd been awake for a few seconds wondering if I'd actually just heard the book play the song, it played again. God seemed to be saying with the second round, "Yes, that was Me, not just your imagination." I believe that God woke me to save me from having a very traumatic nightmare.

At this I awoke and looked around. My sleep had been pleasant to me (Jeremiah 31:26 NIV).

Dear Lord Jesus, please protect and heal my mind. Help me to see where sin or unforgiveness may be causing confusion or chaos. I long to have peace and clarity of mind to enjoy life and to better serve You and others. In Your holy name I pray, amen.

Voices

Have you ever noticed how God's strength and assurance is most clearly on display in your life when you're weak, humble, and vulnerable? When you submit to Him in desperation, becoming completely dependent on Him every moment for comfort and guidance, then He has your invitation and the opportunity to reveal Himself in His glory. He will scatter the enemy on His way to your rescue (Psalm 18:14). Paul's miraculous conversion was accompanied by heavenly revelation. He describes the accompanying demonic spiritual harassment he endured and its surprisingly edifying effect on him:

> The extraordinary level of the revelations I've received is no reason for anyone to exalt me. For this is why a thorn in my flesh was given to me, the Adversary's messenger sent to harass me, keeping me from becoming arrogant. Three times I pleaded with the Lord to relieve me of this. But he answered me, "My grace is always more than enough for you, and my power finds its full expression through your weakness." So I will celebrate my weaknesses, for when I'm weak I sense more deeply the mighty power of Christ living in me (2 Corinthians 12:7-9 TPT).

In 2014, I received visions from the Lord of the numbers 46 and 70 (detailed in the Part II Story, *Visions*). I also heard the Lord say, "The sun will be darkened" (detailed in the Part II story, *Mysteries Unveiled*), and, "I am" (detailed in the Part I story, *I Am*). These revelations from the Lord persuaded me that He's real, He loves me, and that those truths were allowing me to escape a life of unbelief, addiction, and rebellion. With this much victory, the enemy may try a last-ditch effort to intimidate us because he wants to prevent us from following Jesus and experiencing the accompanying peace and joy. I was receiving messages of love and hope from God while simultaneously experiencing sleeplessness because of demonic voices and sounds that only I could hear.

Spiritual harassment from the enemy is intended to drive a person to escape from reality, perhaps with drugs or alcohol. With the help of faith, prayer, and Scripture, I resisted the temptation to use sleep aids and other distractions, although I was often afraid. The enemy only has as much authority in our lives as we give him through sin (Ephesians 4:27), and without authority, he is nothing to fear. Gradually, the attacks became weaker and eventually ceased.

Rather than worry over Satan and his demons, I've learned to focus instead on all the good in my life, like family, health, and obedience to God. As He does with all the enemy's work, God has used the trial for good. When I can't sleep, I pray and forgive others, including myself. As a result, my faith and trust in God has grown tremendously.

> So then, surrender to God. Stand up to the devil and resist him and he will turn and run away from you (James 4:7 TPT).

> *Dear Lord Jesus, please use the enemy's attacks for good, as Your Word promises in Romans 8:28. Please give me the courage to face these trials and this pain without distraction, relying solely on Your love and healing to carry me through. In Your holy name I pray, amen.*

Visions

God sees well ahead into your future, your successes, your inheritances, and your battles. Even as you read this, He may be using these stories to equip you for future struggles. When frightening or uncomfortable situations arise during a season of warfare, you can look back in confidence on what He's taught and revealed to you. As you contend for His kingdom and the war rages around you, remember that in Jesus, you are not condemned.

> And since we are his true children, we qualify to share all his treasures, for indeed, we are heirs of God himself. And since we are joined to Christ, we also inherit all that he is and all that he has. We will experience being co-glorified with him provided that we accept his sufferings as our own (Romans 8:17 TPT).

One autumn morning during a season of intense spiritual warfare, I received a vision from God upon waking one morning. I could clearly see the number "46" in my mind's eye. After some research and waiting, I was led to Psalm 46:10 (TPT): "Surrender your anxiety! Be silent and stop your striving and you will see that I am God. I am the God above all the nations, and I will be exalted throughout the whole earth." The number 46 still holds a special significance for me, as it represents the first time I realized that God will speak directly to us. As with many of God's revelations, this number would also help provide for my family.

Sure enough, the number 46 eventually manifested in a successful investment opportunity: "On Wednesday evening, November 6, Twitter set its initial public offer price….The next morning, Twitter's stock opened at $45.10."[2] I was speaking to the stockbroker that morning when he asked me what price I'd like to limit the transaction at, the highest I'd be willing to pay for the stock. When he confirmed the stock price, I knew $46 was to be my limit price and confirmed the trade.

Several days later, as I was wondering to myself when I should sell our Twitter stock, I received the number 70 clearly in my mind's eye. I began keeping a close eye on the price and sold all my shares as soon as the stock price hit 70 several weeks later on Christmas Eve, which was a Tuesday. That Friday, the stock plummeted and has never recovered. The extra income that Christmas was certainly a blessing. More importantly, the messages from Scripture were timely and comforting. Little did I know how much I needed His protection and deliverance at the time I received these visions.

> Please, Lord! Come quickly and rescue me! God, show me your favor and restore me…But let all who passionately seek you erupt with excitement and joy over what you've done! Let all your lovers, who continually rejoice in the Savior, say aloud, "How great and glorious is our God!" Lord, in my place of weakness and need, won't you turn your heart toward me and hurry to help me? For you are my Savior and I'm always in your thoughts. So don't delay to deliver me now, for you are my God (Psalm 70:1, 4-5 TPT).

> *Dear Lord Jesus, thank You for equipping me for the battles ahead, giving me the spiritual armor necessary to defeat giants. Help me to grasp the spiritual significance of Your gifts and revelations. In Your holy name I pray, amen.*

---

2. Steve Schaefer, "Twitter Stock Pops In NYSE Debut, Finishes First Day With 73% Gain," Forbes Online, Posted November 7, 2013, accessed October 25, 2019, https://www.forbes.com/sites/steveschaefer/2013/11/07/twitter-opens-at-45-10-stock-pops-73-in-nyse-debut/#25e9449422d8

SOZO

God knows how much you need other people during times of crisis. He understands that you need to share your story with a wise and compassionate soul. Please understand that some people in ministry are more trustworthy and helpful than others. Pray for the Lord's guidance before you seek counseling. He will lead you to someone with His heart for helping others without judgment and condemnation.

> For wherever two or three come together in honor of my
> name, I am right there with them! (Matthew 18:20 TPT).

Sozo is the Greek word translated "to save, keep safe and sound, to rescue from danger or destruction."[3] It was early January 2014, and I was debating whether I should participate in the Sozo ministry available at some charismatic churches. It was highly recommended to me by a Christian friend and mentor, but I still had my doubts because it requires one to discuss fairly intimate life details and memories with a small group of church leaders as part of the healing process. Gradually God revealed His will in several different ways to let me know that I should participate. First, I received a Bible-verse-of-the-day message with Matthew 18:20, noted above.

The next way God confirmed His will was through the number five, which has been one of God's numbers for me. It means "grace," so it follows that fifty-five is indicative of "double grace." There was no charge to make the Sozo ministry appointment, but a fifty-five dollar donation was suggested. Isaiah 55 is a call for those who need help to cry out to God, an invitation to the thirsty: "Listen! Are you thirsty for

---

3. "Greek Lexicon entry for Sozo," Bible Study Tools Online, accessed December 12, 2019, https://www.biblestudytools.com/lexicons/greek/nas/sozo.html

more? Come to the refreshing waters and drink. Even if you have no money, come, buy, and eat…it won't cost a thing" (Isaiah 55:1 TPT). Once we accept Jesus as Lord and Savior and ask Him for help, He will pardon our sins free of charge. Jesus has already paid our way.

I decided to try Sozo ministry. I arrived at the church, and the facilitators led prayer and some discussion regarding what had brought me there. Although I was hesitant to discuss much during my first appointment, I had a much better experience the second time I went. Throughout the process, God highlighted the importance of relying on Him first, then trusting other people in the healing process. I'd had it backwards, seeking answers from people first. We have direct access to the Father through Jesus by way of prayer, trust, and faith.

> Seek the Lord Yahweh when he makes himself approachable; call upon him when you sense he is near. The wicked need to abandon their ways, and sinful ones need to banish every evil thought. Let them return to Yahweh, and they will experience his compassionate mercy. Yes, let them return to God, for he will lavish forgiveness upon them (Isaiah 55:6-7 TPT).

Dear Lord Jesus, thank You for the gift of discernment and the sweet way You call us to look out for each other. Please remind me to seek guidance from You first, and then trust Your followers to help me too. In Your holy name I pray, amen.

Slave No More

Do you have habits you know you'd be better off without? Is there anything that frequently brings you temporary pleasure, only to be followed by shame, guilt, or regret? Who or what do you first turn to for comfort, if not God? The first of the Ten Commandments says we shall have no other gods but the one, true God. It's found in the third verse of Exodus 20: "You shall have no other gods before Me" (AMP). Although our enemy, satan, fully intends to ensnare and enslave us any way he can, God doesn't intend for you to be a slave in any form, including the bondage of addiction.

> One Sabbath day, while Jesus was teaching in the synagogue, he encountered a seriously handicapped woman. She was crippled and had been doubled over for eighteen years. Her condition was caused by a demonic spirit of bondage that had left her unable to stand up straight. When Jesus saw her condition, he called her over and gently laid his hands on her. Then he said, "Dear woman, you are free. I release you forever from this crippling spirit." Instantly she stood straight and tall and overflowed with glorious praise to God! (Luke 13:10-13 TPT).

During the few weeks following the stormy morning when I heard the Lord say "I Am," the number eighteen began to appear to me everywhere—written on the sidewalk, on signage, and in books. Eighteen symbolizes freedom from physical and spiritual bondage in Scripture, as illustrated in the story of Jesus healing the handicapped woman. The story reminds me of the struggle I had when overcoming my addiction to exercise, including yoga—which often has participants bending into the various postures and can be an addictive form of demon worship.

David spoke the words of Psalm 18 to the Lord when God delivered him from the hand of all his enemies, including Goliath and the Philistines, and later from the hand of Israel's King Saul. The chapter (verses 13-14 in particular) outlines what was happening in the spirit realm during the thunderstorm when He spoke to me. My enemies attacked when I was at my weakest, struggling with anorexia and insomnia while raising a toddler. God revealed Himself and sent His heavenly host of angels to help as I battled for my health, family, and freedom.

> The Lord thundered, the great God above every god spoke with his thunder-voice from the skies. What fearsome hailstones and flashes of fire were before him! He released his lightning-arrows, and routed my foes. See how they ran and scattered in fear! Then with his mighty roar he laid bare the foundations of the earth, uncovering the secret source of the sea. The hidden depths of land and sea were exposed by the hurricane-blast of his hot breath. He then reached down from heaven, all the way from the sky to the sea. He reached down into my darkness to rescue me! He took me out of my calamity and chaos and drew me to himself, taking me from the depths of my despair! Even though I was helpless in the hands of my hateful, strong enemy, you were good to deliver me. When I was at my weakest, my enemies attacked—but the Lord held on to me. His love broke open the way and he brought me into a beautiful broad place. He rescued me—because his delight is in me! (Psalm 18:13-19 TPT).

Dear Lord Jesus, thank You for rescuing and delivering me from destruction. Bad habits in my life quickly turn into dangerous idols that I can't escape from on my own. Please give me discernment to avoid similar traps in the future. In Your holy name I pray, amen.

Free of Debt

God cares for every detail of your life, including your personal finances. He's not mad when you overspend or accumulate debt, He only wants to help you get financially healthy. After all, He gave us godly men like Dave Ramsey who have great knowledge about finances and how to get free from debt! Just like other areas of your life, God's not counting your mistakes against you. He doesn't oversee a debtor's prison. Jesus already paid your debt—including the monetary kind. Don't be surprised when your tithing brings great blessing.

> If you borrow money with interest, you'll end up serving the interests of your creditors, for the rich rule over the poor (Proverbs 22:7 TPT).

Since Nick and I began tithing in 2010, we have seen miracles happen in our finances. I have so many awesome stories about God's provision in our lives that I could probably write a separate book on just that facet of His love. Only five years after Nick and I purchased our first home, its value had appreciated significantly. We sold it and used the profit to pay off my student loans, our credit card debt, and two car loans. We also pre-paid for most of a two-week family vacation to Hawaii.

We put our second house on the market in July of 2018. After having two more sweet babies since buying it in 2016, we had already outgrown its three bedrooms! We got an offer on the first day of Rosh Hashanah, a holiday celebrating the Jewish New Year and new beginnings. The Lord is faithful to expand our surroundings to accommodate growth (2 Kings 6:1-2) and is kind to appoint universal times to wipe clean our slates, including debt.

With the proceeds from the sale, we again paid off our debt, including another car loan, debt from home upgrades, a credit card, and much of our outstanding income tax. Today, with no mortgage looming over us, we are dreaming of and planning for our forever home, which will be built in God's perfect timing. Debt is surely a form of bondage that Scripture warns about and discourages, and God loves to erase it. With Jesus, we also experience personal forgiveness whenever we ask.

> Every fiftieth year, on the Day of Atonement, let the trumpets blow loud and long throughout the land. For the fiftieth year shall be holy, a time to proclaim liberty throughout the land to all enslaved debtors, and a time for the canceling of all public and private debts. It shall be a year when all the family estates sold to others shall be returned to the original owners or their heirs. What a happy year it will be! In it you shall not sow, nor gather crops nor grapes; for it is a holy Year of Jubilee for you. That year your food shall be the volunteer crops that grow wild in the fields. Yes, during the Year of Jubilee everyone shall return home to his original family possession; if he has sold it, it shall be his again! (Leviticus 25:8-13 TLB).

Dear Lord Jesus, thank You for getting me out of dire financial situations. Instead of dread, I now joyfully anticipate the future. I'm secure in your blessings and the promises of those to come. Please give me plenty of opportunities to help others who struggle financially. In Your holy name I pray, amen.

Renewing of the Mind

You can look just about anywhere and find ads, social media posts, and articles about self-improvement. Entire industries are devoted to "helping you" maintain the appearance of your body and home. We are inundated with messages like: "eat this," "do this exercise," "clean with this," or "organize like this." It is important to understand the benefits of a clean home and physical exercise, but please don't sacrifice your health or time with loved ones to achieve these short-term goals.

> Stop imitating the ideals and opinions of the culture around you, but be inwardly transformed by the Holy Spirit through a total reformation of how you think. This will empower you to discern God's will as you live a beautiful life, satisfying and perfect in his eyes (Romans 12:2 TPT).

Frequent yoga and running helped me lose weight quickly after I gave birth to our first son, Jackson. But it was only a year or so into my routine when I became quite weak and bony. Because of its addictive nature, it was extremely difficult for me to stop the excessive exercise. God woke me up—quite literally. I was unable to sleep well for the first half of 2014 as I read and searched and prayed for deliverance. The Lord had to convince me that caring for my children was my primary responsibility, always taking priority over achieving and maintaining a beautiful home and body.

After Evelyn was born, I quickly became exhausted from the combination of caring for a newborn and her two big brothers, housekeeping (with a puppy), and meal preparation. I experienced intense pain in my lower back when I would overdo it. I would often cry at the thought of getting out of bed because the pain would be unbearable. Sometimes I despaired that I would be handicapped at an early age. For many months it didn't occur to me that I simply needed more rest.

One day the Lord revealed to me in His Word that He gives His people rest (Exodus 33:14 NKJV), so I began the habit of napping whenever I got the opportunity. I reduced my caffeine intake and eventually quit drinking coffee, and began living life more slowly. I also completed intensive therapy with a chiropractor to heal my rotated hips. I've experienced almost total healing. I still use my back as a gauge for physical activity, although it takes much longer for it to begin aching and I don't have any debilitating pain.

God showed me how valuable I am to my family. He freed me from thinking that I need to exercise in order to look perfect or that I need to compensate for "not working" by doing excessive housework. He has shown me that I need regular rest and therapy to recover from illness or injury, it's okay to seek help with the kids, house, or anything else that I can't do in an emotionally and physically healthy manner. It's wonderful to finally be able to see some things from His perspective and understand my value as a wife and mom.

> The Lord does not look at the things people look at. People look at the outward appearance, but the Lord looks at the heart (1 Samuel 16:7 NIV).

> *Dear Lord Jesus, thank You for healing me and delivering me from a grueling daily routine. Thank You for showing me how to spend slow, quality time with my family in an imperfect home and body. Thank You for providing the resources I need to occasionally outsource work, giving me time for Your precious healing rest. In Your holy name I pray, amen.*

The Cloud and Pillar

The next time you're outdoors, take some time to fully appreciate the world God created. Hear His birds, feel His breeze, and gaze at His sky. Observe how all of creation is constantly responding to His presence. His existence is always evident to anyone with eyes and ears, but He can choose to manifest in more powerful and unusual ways. He may want to guide you, shake you, calm you, or simply hug you through the power of His Holy Spirit.

> That is how it continued to be; the cloud covered it, and at night it looked like fire. Whenever the cloud lifted from above the tent, the Israelites set out; wherever the cloud settled, the Israelites encamped. At the Lord's command the Israelites set out, and at his command they encamped. As long as the cloud stayed over the tabernacle, they remained in camp (Numbers 9:16-18 NIV).

During the hard January of 2014 when I was plagued with unwanted spiritual visitors, I visited the local First Baptist Church. I must have been expecting to receive a quick deliverance and skip away happily. When I told the secretary what I was experiencing, she suggested that I go to the hospital. Then one of the pastors prayed with me and expressed sympathy, although he had no experience with deliverance. He said a group of sixty to seventy people would pray for me that evening.

I believe God heard all the prayers, including mine, and acknowledged my act of submission and faith. I began to experience a process of healing and restoration. He healed me and my relationships so I could move forward in glorifying Him and doing

His will, including helping others to accept Jesus into their hearts and receive salvation.

The pastor also gave me a book of devotions titled *A Daybook of Grace* published by Fall River Press. Each daily devotion proved relevant to my life during that season. God spoke to me through them and used them to guide me to additional scriptures. One day the devotional referenced Numbers 9. In the same way that the Israelites looked to the cloud over God's tabernacle to know if they should stay put in the desert or pack up and keep going, God had called me to wake up from my spiritual numbness and follow Him where He wanted me to go.

Not long afterward, I was talking with someone about the amazing signs and miracles Bill Johnson, senior leader of Bethel Church in Redding, California, had witnessed. So this person and I watched a video of Bill describing a "glory cloud" of light and smoke that appeared above some worshippers one day during a service he was leading. As I listened to Bill describe it, I thought immediately of my devotional and God's cloud of guidance that appeared to the Israelites. It is no coincidence that the devotional and Bill's video referred to clouds of God's physical presence. God was confirming Bill's story for me.

From that point on, I had no doubts about attending Bethel Church in Tyrone, Georgia. The heavy anointing and deliverance ministry there helped me get through a dark time. God was also working in the heart of the person I watched the video with. God's signs and miracles enrich not only our lives as believers, but the lives of those who need salvation and the good news of Jesus. If we seek Him we will find Him!

> And I will not be presumptuous to speak of anything except what Christ has accomplished through me. For many non-Jewish people are coming into faith's obedience by the power of the Spirit of God, which is displayed through mighty signs and amazing wonders,

both in word and deed. Starting from Jerusalem I went from place to place as far as the distant Roman province of Illyricum, fully preaching the wonderful message of Christ (Romans 15:18-19 TPT).

Dear Lord Jesus, thank You for allowing me the occasional glimpse of Your signs and wonders. The beauty and love in all You do, draws me nearer to You. Thank You for guiding me through the wilderness. Please give me continual evidence of Your power and existence as a beacon to the lost. In Your holy name I pray, amen.

In Tents

We all must wander at some point in order to learn, heal, forgive, and eventually find the path the Lord has established for us. You may be in a season of desert wandering right now. Living in literal or figurative shelters before the Lord establishes you to live out your permanent calling. You are delivered and purified in the desert seasons. You learn to depend on Him for your every need, and He reveals to you glimpses of your promised land flowing with milk and honey.

> We are convinced that even if these bodies we live in are folded up at death like tents, we will still have a God-built home that no human hands have built, which will last forever in the heavenly realm. We inwardly sigh *as we live in these physical "tents,"* longing to put on a new body for our life in heaven, in the belief that once we put on our new "clothing" we won't find ourselves "naked." So, while living in this "tent," we groan under its burden, not because we want to die but because we want these new bodies. We crave for all that is mortal to be swallowed up by *eternal* life. *And this is no empty hope*, for God himself is the one who has prepared us for this wonderful destiny. And to confirm this promise, he has given us the Holy Spirit, like an engagement ring, as a guarantee (2 Corinthians 5:1-5 TPT).

I wandered for thirty-five years—nearly as long as the Israelites wandered in the desert, living in tents, before the Lord led them into the promised land. I wandered because I didn't know the Lord until I was thirty-one years old. It's 2020 and I've also not yet settled into a permanent physical home. When I was a child, our family bought and sold a house every five years or so. I rented houses in college. And while I love the neighborhood we currently live in, my husband and I are still renting a house. We live in the fourth home we've rented together.

As with any adventure, wandering can be fun. In 2017, we embarked on a major home renovation due to severe water damage in several areas of the home we owned. We spent weeks in nice hotels and rental homes, all courtesy of our insurance company. My kids and I went on daily urban excursions to playgrounds, eateries, and museums. Insurance even covered all of our meals, so cooking was not required. We enjoyed plenty of quality family time, and the end result of the renovation was beautiful.

Under President Donald Trump, a Christian, the US is enjoying a season of peace, stability, prosperity, and freedom. His presidency was heralded by major celestial events during the previous desert season. The Jewish holiday of Sukkot (Feast of Tabernacles/Tents) coincided with two of the four back-to-back red supermoons in 2014-2015. And the total solar eclipse of August 21, 2017, was the first in the US since 1979. God can use anything to communicate with us, but celestial bodies were created for that specifically (Genesis 1:14). I look back and see the correlation between my own deliverance, the end of my wandering, and the major celestial events that have taken place since early 2014. I've since discovered God and experienced the purification, deliverance, and revelation that inevitably follows.

> So we are convinced that every detail of our lives is continually woven together to fit into God's perfect plan of bringing good into our lives, for we are his lovers who have been called to fulfill his designed purpose (Romans 8:28 TPT).

Dear Lord Jesus, thank You for comforting me and reminding me of Your promises during my wandering desert season. Help me see Your grace and provision when it seems difficult. Thank You for the adventures and glimpses of the future that are sprinkled along the journey. In Your holy name I pray, amen.

A Glimpse of the Promised Land

In His perfect timing, God will reveal to you the details of your future. He may use a prophet or prophetess to seek you out. You may have an epiphany in broad daylight. You may even dream vividly of His plans for you while you sleep. Though He may warn you of danger, heavenly revelation will most often be promising, uplifting, and encouraging.

> This is what I will do in the last days—I will pour out my Spirit on everybody and cause your sons and daughters to prophesy, and your young men will see visions, and your old men will experience dreams *from God* (Acts 2:17 TPT).

I had two dreams in 2018 just after we'd had our fourth child, Nick Jr., and just before we put our older three-bedroom house on the market. I dreamt of my present and future in the same night. In one dream I saw myself in the house we lived in, lying paralyzed. Nick's landscape crew had applied herbicide in our yard and I was poisoned. This was God's warning about staying in our tiny house with a big mortgage. As long as we were pouring everything we made into the mortgage and maintenance on our old house, we would have little freedom to pursue our dreams. We weren't progressing toward our creative self-employment goals of writing, homebuilding, and homeschooling—because when in debt, every dollar made is already allocated to someone else.

In the second dream Nick said to me, "I'm going to carry on the work my Dad did, but I'm going to *build* the houses because the labor is so cheap." When I told him about it, Nick laughed at the cheap labor cost detail. It probably seems out of place to anyone familiar with homebuilding. After he'd had a moment to process it, he made the connection between cheap labor and *prefabricated* homes. Prior to this dream, we'd often discussed their appeal. I'd presented on them in graduate school about eight years prior. Unlike traditional homebuilding that can take years and untold man-hours to complete, prefabricated homes are delivered in large sections and erected in a matter of weeks, sometimes just days.

Nick's employment elsewhere hurts sometimes, hence the possible reason his landscape crew was in the first dream. We live different lives all day long and try to reconcile everything at 5:00 p.m. I don't think that's what God intended for families. I look forward to the day when we're both self-employed and working on the same team. In God's perfect timing, we will begin our venture developing small tracts of land with prefabricated homes.

> "For I know the plans I have for you," declares the Lord, "plans to prosper you and not to harm you, plans to give you hope and a future. Then you will call on me and come and pray to me, and I will listen to you. You will seek me and find me when you seek me with all your heart" (Jeremiah 29:11-13 NIV).

> *Dear Lord Jesus, thank You for revealing to me glimpses of my future. Please help me stay on the path You've prepared for me, unwavering and uncompromising. Help me seek You and discern Your plans for me. In Your holy name I pray, amen.*

Onward

Are you being led into a new beginning, into an exciting place of prosperity and freedom? If you sense God is leading you into a new reality, then pursue His calling with all your might! Do not let fear of leaving the familiar beckon you backward. You've outgrown your surroundings and need a new wineskin.

> And who would pour fresh, new wine into an old wineskin? Eventually the wine will ferment and make the wineskin burst, losing everything—the wine is spilled and the wineskin ruined. Instead, new wine is always poured into a new wineskin so that both are preserved (Matthew 9:17 TPT).

The second house we owned did not sell quickly. After about a month with no offers, Nick suggested we take it off the market for a while. He wanted to list it again after a few months so it would be freshly posted and hopefully sell within a few weeks.

I was vehemently opposed, as I'd already prepped and vacated the house for showings countless times with our four kids, including a newborn. Each time someone wanted to see it, I'd pick up all the toys, make all the beds, clean off the counters, get every kid dressed, light a candle, crate the dog, and herd everyone into the car for a trip to who knows where.

I was tired and ready to accept the first offer to just be done with it. How could he expect me and the kids to do it all over again? Couldn't we just sell the house that was too tiny for us and move on with our lives? Why take two steps forward toward freedom only to take one step back toward bondage?

Thank God we didn't take the house off the market, because we got an offer soon afterward. A couple and their realtor were driving down our street and decided to stop in. We weren't ready for them—it was a total surprise! They immediately loved the house and began working on their offer. We found out they are also Christian believers and felt the house had a sweet spirit. They needed a house and our family needed rest. Sometimes the Promised Land is right around the corner. God is faithful!

The Bible says as the Israelites approached the Promised Land, there were times when they felt too uncomfortable or afraid of the unknown to progress toward the wonderful things God had planned for them. They grumbled about not having as much to eat as they'd had in captivity in Egypt (Exodus 16:3). The spies they sent in, returned with a bad report about the land—even while holding evidence of the land's fruit (Numbers 13:32). They wanted to avoid moving forward.

Only Joshua and Caleb gave an accurate report of the land. For their obedience and truthfulness, Joshua and Caleb were allowed to progress into Canaan, while the rest of their generation was sentenced to continue wandering in the desert until all of them had died. Faith takes risks for the sake of obedience.

> The land we passed through and explored is exceedingly good. If the Lord is pleased with us, he will lead us into that land, a land flowing with milk and honey, and will give it to us. Only do not rebel against the Lord. And do not be afraid of the people of the land, because we will devour them. Their protection is gone, but the Lord is with us. Do not be afraid of them (Numbers 14:7 NIV).

> *Dear Lord Jesus, thank You for a new reality. You are constantly renewing my heart, my circumstances, and my perspective. Help me to recognize Your invitations to pursue You into the unknown Promised Land. In Your holy name I pray, amen.*

Breakthrough

reakthroughs aren't always easy. There are heavenly forces at work moving you along, lining up the right people and circumstances. There are also dark forces at work to derail you, attempting to offend and frighten you. Keeping your eyes fixed on Jesus is the only way to get through tempestuous times.

> I will surely gather all of you, Jacob; I will surely bring together the remnant of Israel. I will bring them together like sheep in a pen, like a flock in its pasture; the place will throng with people. The One who breaks open the way will go up before them; they will break through the gate and go out. Their King will pass through before them, the Lord at their head (Micah 2:12-13 NIV).

We knew we'd found our homebuyers once they made an offer, although working with them wasn't always easy. They missed some deadlines, had lots of questions about the house every step of the way, and requested a change in the closing date at least five times. They just weren't experienced in basic real estate transaction etiquette. We gave them grace though, because that's how one operates whose eyes are fixed on the Holy One. And it paid off in the end.

Free at last, free at last, thank God Almighty we were free at last! Once the sale was finalized, we paid off our mortgage, the home's new HVAC system, and the full-sized vehicle upgrade to transport four kids. It is amazing how much more money it feels like we have with little to zero debt. One day we'll be in a position to purchase a home up front with no loan. For now, we have freed up our cash flow to feed, house, clothe, and entertain four precious little people. We also have time to plan our new home.

Nick recently asked me to describe my dream home. Naively, I began with an online quiz including questions about the facade, architecture, and furniture styles. Then I realized that regardless of what the house looks like, it won't stand unless it's built by God. So, rethinking my answer, I arrived at this description: My dream home is built by the Lord (Psalm 127:1) on a rock (Matthew 7:24-27) with wisdom and understanding (Proverbs 24:3). It has a beautiful view of God's majestic creation. It's exactly what He has planned for us, fitting perfectly in our budget (Deuteronomy 15:6) in a timeless style to pass down through the generations (Proverbs 13:22). It will be peaceful, secure, and quiet (Isaiah 32:18) and a place for us to dwell forever (1 Kings 8:13). Praise the Lord, our Master Builder, for His mercy, wisdom, and kindness!

> But during the night, the Lord sent an angel *who appeared before them*. He supernaturally opened their prison doors and brought the apostles outside. "Go," the angel told them. "Stand in the temple courts and preach the words that bring life!" (Acts 5:19-20 TPT).

> *Dear Lord Jesus, thank You for miraculous breakthrough. You promise to set the captives free, and that's exactly what You've done for me and my family. Please help me to avoid the enemy's traps to entangle me, and give me the opportunity to help others find freedom and breakthrough. In Your holy name I pray, amen.*

The Scarlet Cord

Pray for those you love, and they will be helped, even if they haven't accepted Jesus as Lord and Savior. When you ask Jesus into your life, your family is also covered by the blood of Jesus. When you sign up, He gives you the family plan at no cost! Your spouse is saved, and your children are protected. Imagine the Lord holding a divine umbrella over your household, shielding you all from life's storms.

> They answered, "Believe in the Lord Jesus and you will be saved—*you and all your family.*" Then they prophesied the word of the Lord over him and all his family. Even though the hour was late, he washed their wounds. Then he and all his family were baptized. He took Paul and Silas into his home and set them at his table and fed them. The jailer and all his family were filled with joy in their newfound faith in God (Acts 16:31-34 TPT).

I once heard Franklin Jentezen explain that Rahab's scarlet cord represented Jesus' blood sacrifice and gift of eternal life even before He walked the earth. The Israeli spies in Jericho formed an alliance with her for hiding them in her home. As the spies departed for their camp to report back and get ready for the attack, they instructed her to hang a scarlet cord from her window during the invasion so the army could identify and protect her and her family. By choosing the God of the Israelites and the scarlet cord, her entire pagan household was also saved.

Nick first accepted Jesus as His Lord and Savior the day God spared our baby Evelyn's life when drywall from our rain-soaked ceiling landed in her crib. Any doubts I had about God's sovereignty were also removed then. The good Lord reached down and preserved our entire family that day. I surely would have perished along with my daughter had any harm come to her.

Since I chose Jesus, I've received a new life. Others in my family have been saved. We've been delivered from death, oppression, debt, and a slave mentality. We've dreamed dreams and seen visions, we've conquered giants and entered their territory for the taking. We've been through hell, come out whole on the other side, and are marching around the walls of Jericho. His grace runs through our lives like the scarlet cord—and did so even before we believed.

> But Christ proved God's passionate love for us by dying in our place while we were still lost and ungodly! And there is still much more to say of his unfailing love for us! For through the blood of Jesus we have heard the powerful declaration, "You are now righteous in my sight." And because of the sacrifice of Jesus, you will never experience the wrath of God (Romans 5:8-9 TPT).

> *Dear Lord Jesus, thank You for loving me even before I knew You. You've rescued me from destruction and preserved those dearest to me. I can never repay You, but I will tell others of Your grace and goodness. In Your holy name I pray, amen.*

Part 3:

Inheritance

The lines have fallen for me in pleasant places; indeed, I have a beautiful inheritance.

Psalm 16:6 ESV

Humble Beginnings

God asks for a tithe, a gift given freely and regularly to others—especially to His children who are in need. He doesn't ask for anything because He needs it. He asks for it to build your faith. Would you be willing to give your last ten dollars away and trust that God will provide everything you need after you've emptied your wallet in obedience to Him? He doesn't mince words with His promise to keep His end of the deal.

> Bring the whole tithe into the storehouse, that there may be food in my house. "Test me in this," says the Lord Almighty, "and see if I will not throw open the floodgates of heaven and pour out so much blessing that there will not be room enough to store it" (Malachi 3:10 NIV).

My husband and I began tithing in 2010 by following the rule in the Old Testament that requires a regular gift equaling ten percent of our income (Deuteronomy 14:22-23). I didn't know a better way because I had yet to grasp that as a Christian every action should flow from relationship rather than rules. Fortunately, God honors a tithe regardless of the method. The same year we began tithing we welcomed Jackson, our first child, into the world. We were faithful to tithe, and God gave us the desire of our hearts (Psalm 37:4).

We have since seen miracles happen in our finances that we know were orchestrated by God. One Christmas we racked up $2,310 in credit card charges to cover some unexpected travel expenses. Upon returning home from Hawaii in January, I received a bonus check from my employer in the amount of $2,310 and was able to pay off the credit card immediately. Yes, the dollar amount of the check was the same as the dollar amount owed!

Our tithing today looks much different than it did when we started, as we don't calculate the ten percent. Instead, our giving is directed by our relationship with the Lord. He reveals opportunities to give generously to someone in need; we rarely have to look for them anymore. We need only remember that His guidelines for giving tend to prioritize providing for the poor (Deuteronomy 15:10-11), starting with fellow Christian believers (Galatians 6:10), widows, and orphans (James 1:27). If we give everyone what they ask for, we will easily exceed the ten percent tithe and build beautiful relationships in the process. I remember not being able to comprehend this promise when we struggled financially, because I was so accustomed to the world's way—save, save, save, not give, give, give. God's way is always more fun!

> Learn to generously share what you have with those who ask for help, and don't close your heart to the one who comes to borrow from you (Matthew 5:42 TPT).

> *Dear Lord Jesus, thank You for Your sovereignty in my life, including financial matters. Please continue to guide me to those in need, especially widows, orphans, and fellow believers. Help me not to overlook anyone who asks of me. I understand You'll pour blessings into my life when I hold nothing back from You. In Your holy name I pray, amen.*

Show Hospitality to Strangers

Be kind to everyone. Not only are some angels disguised as people, but it pleases God when we bless and empathize with others, regardless of how deserving we believe they are. We are not without fault, and we don't know the whole story surrounding someone's private struggles, so err on the side of love and generosity. You will receive the sweetest blessings from people who just need a few dollars for a drink or a meal. They are grateful no matter the size of the gift.

> And show hospitality to strangers, for they may be angels
> from God showing up as your guests (Hebrews 13:2 TPT).

One day during my season of heavy spiritual warfare in 2014, I was working from home when the doorbell rang. I opened it to find a well-dressed young man holding a binder and asking for support with his education. If I would purchase magazines from him, he could finish school and better support his wife and newborn daughter.

I recognized God's confirmation when the man stated that the price for the magazine subscription was fifty-five dollars, as He often uses the numbers five and fifty-five to communicate with me. Further, I recalled Hebrews 13:2 that encourages kindness and hospitality toward strangers. Between those two affirmations, along with the arm bracelet the young man was wearing that said "I am second," and his professed love of Jesus, I was persuaded to purchase the magazines.

That evening, panic struck me and I became so anxious that I could barely enjoy dinner. I could not help but worry our bank account was somehow going to be compromised and drained because I'd given a personal check to a stranger. Nick was not particularly concerned and his calmness transferred to me, so I decided to pray and sleep on it.

The next day I opened a daily devotional and the topic was "Moving Forward." My worry vanished as I remembered the name of the young man's school was also "Moving Forward." God was again gracefully affirming His hand in the matter and encouraging my trust in Him. Our bank account was not compromised and the check cleared within the week.

> Don't be pulled in different directions or worried about a thing. Be saturated in prayer throughout each day, offering your faith-filled requests before God with overflowing gratitude. Tell him every detail of your life, then God's wonderful peace that transcends human understanding, *will make the answers known to you* through Jesus Christ (Philippians 4:6-7 TPT).

> *Dear Lord Jesus, thank You for opportunities to show kindness to others—even angels. Help me always be quick to listen when approached by anyone asking for help. Please give me peace in uncertainty, and discernment and compassion for those in need. In Your holy name I pray, amen.*

Unbridled Grace

Have you ever witnessed someone fall from grace, only to see them make an extraordinary comeback (think Martha Stewart, Tiger Woods, Donald Trump)? The Lord doles out grace to everyone—even the ones you might think deserve punishment. This can be rather frustrating when you are seeking justice, but oh so sweet when you are on the receiving end of an unexpected pardon or unmerited favorable outcome. You will be blessed—not disappointed—when you also lift up those the world has condemned. Even when you're angry with someone, pray for them and trust the Lord's justice to manifest in beautiful and unexpected ways and in His timing.

> Your ancestors have also been taught "Love your neighbors and hate the one who hates you." However, I say to you, love your enemy, bless the one who curses you, do something wonderful for the one who hates you, and respond to the very ones who persecute you by praying for them. For that will reveal your identity as children of your heavenly Father. He is kind to all by bringing the sunrise to warm and rainfall to refresh whether a person does what is good or evil. What reward do you deserve if you only love the loveable? Don't even the tax collectors do that? How are you any different from others if you limit your kindness only to your friends? Don't even the ungodly do that? Since you are children of a perfect Father in heaven, you are to be perfect like him (Matthew 5:43-48 TPT).

The Lord is perfect, His justice is perfect, and His treatment of His children is perfect. He rewards people, even the undeserving, with kindness under our new covenant with Him (Hebrews 7:22; 8:7). He does this in order to draw the lost to him (Romans 2:4) because His thoughts are higher than ours and His ways higher than ours (Isaiah 55:8-9). Sometimes I imagine God as the officer who pulls a car over only to discover that the driver has young children who are not riding in car seats as required by law. Instead of writing the driver a ticket, the officer escorts them to the nearest superstore and buys new car seats for the children.

God has set the standard of perfection for our behavior, which leaves no room for unforgiveness, prejudice, or ill-will toward anyone. God forgives others just as quickly as He forgives us (Psalm 103:8) and is pleased when we quickly forgive those who have hurt us. Jesus defines perfection in us not by what we have, how we look, or what we can accomplish for ourselves, but by how we treat others, especially those the world would dispense with. He says perfection is achieved when our kindness has no limit, like the Father's. We achieve perfection not by striving, but through our love toward everyone, including the most unlikely recipients.

> Do not seek revenge or bear a grudge against anyone among your people, but love your neighbor as yourself. I am the Lord (Leviticus 19:18 NIV).

> Never gloat when your enemy meets disaster and don't be quick to rejoice if he falls. For the Lord, who sees your heart, will be displeased with you and will pity your foe (Proverbs 24:17-18 TPT).

> *Dear Lord Jesus, thank You for setting the perfect example of how to treat our enemies. Please give me the wisdom to forgive and bless those who hurt me, the courage to defend the defenseless, and the discernment to understand the difference. In Your holy name I pray, amen.*

Little Children

If you've accepted Jesus as Lord and Savior, you have a new identity as His child. You haven't earned His unconditional love, but He gives it freely—and did so even before you loved Him. He's also given you free will along with the *choice* to love Him in return, because forced love is not love at all. He's overjoyed when you love Him back.

> Yet to all who did receive him, to those who believed in his name, he gave the right to become children of God—children born not of natural descent, nor of human decision or a husband's will, but born of God (John 1:12-13 NIV).

We can see the Father's grace, beauty, and kindness in other people, especially children. After all, He speaks in a still, small voice (1 Kings 19:12 NKJV). When my children hold up their little hands to be picked up, ask for something, or show me the toy they're so proud of, I know the love and attention I give them in those moments is love I'm showing to God (Matthew 18:5). I'm never closer to Him than when I'm holding them, smelling their hair, kissing their foreheads, and looking into their beautiful eyes.

When I acknowledge and attempt to grant the many requests of my children each day, God leads me through a treasure hunt to find and stay in His beautiful presence. When they approach me, I have to put down my smartphone or close the computer and give them my full attention. Then they're more likely to plop down in my lap or recline against me, and they talk longer if I make eye contact. This is also how our heavenly Father responds to us: "Move your heart closer and closer to God, and he will come even closer to you" (James 4:8 TPT).

Children assign value to activities, things, and people (including themselves) based on their parents' values. They determine what is important by studying the choices made by the adults in their lives. Anything I would give priority to over the Lord and His command to feed His lambs becomes an idol and a stumbling block for me and my children. I struggle with being fully present for my kids while responding to e-mails and messages, reading books, and soaking in inspirational posts and videos. If I don't pour myself out to my children, they tend to turn away to playing on their tablets, eating junk food, and even manifesting aggressiveness toward their siblings. I must demonstrate to my children that they're my priceless priority. This way they will never feel unloved or unwelcome and they will learn to value themselves and the good things of God (Matthew 6:21).

> Whoever welcomes a little child in my name welcomes me. And whoever welcomes me welcomes not only me, but the one who sent me (Mark 9:37 TPT).

> But Jesus called for the parents, the children, and his disciples to come and listen to him. Then he told them, "Never hinder a child from coming to me. Let them all come, for God's kingdom realm belongs to them as much as it does to anyone else. *They demonstrate to you what faith is all about*" (Luke 18:16 TPT).

> *Dear Lord Jesus, thank You for the wonderful blessing of children. Help me not take them for granted for even a second. Please give me patience, time, resources, and wisdom to make them feel loved and special, and to teach them all they need to know. Please continue to watch over them. In Your holy name I pray, amen.*

A Deposit

Don't worry about how you will share the gospel. God knows your strengths and weaknesses and will provide you with the right tools and opportunities. You don't have to be Billy Graham to give someone hope and point them to Christ. Look for the hurting and approach them kindly with the simple, beautiful message of the cross.

> For this is how much God loved the world—he gave his one and only, unique Son as a gift. So now everyone who believes in him will never perish but experience everlasting life. God did not send his Son into the world to judge and condemn the world, but to be its Savior and rescue it! So now there is no longer any condemnation for those who believe in him, but the unbeliever already lives under condemnation because they do not believe in the name of God's beloved Son (John 3:16-18 TPT).

It was January 2013, and I was cleaning the house—accomplishing post-Christmas decoration take-down. As I lifted the seat cushion on the sofa to vacuum there, I noticed a small, round object about the size of a nickel under the cushion. It wasn't of great physical quality, probably just a piece of plastic with metallic paint. It was decorated with a cross and "John 3:16" was printed on it. I had not seen it before and imagined that it was a small token from God, just to say hello. I displayed it in my son Jackson's room and it hung from his bulletin board for several months.

Later in the year, I learned that an acquaintance I had known for many years was not a Christian believer. Soon afterward, God reminded me of the token as a way to send His message of love. When God was commissioning Moses to free the Israelites from Pharaoh's oppression, He said to Moses, "What is that in your hand?" Moses replied, "A staff." God used what Moses already had in his possession to get a message of hope and freedom to the Israelites living under Pharaoh's oppression in Egypt (Exodus 4:2 NIV).

I carried the token with me on a few occasions when I expected to see my unbelieving friend, hoping for a covert way to leave it with them. They didn't need to know where it came from, only what was written on it. Also, I didn't want it to seem that they were just being given a tiny piece of junk as a gift or being preached at, so I decided it should be found by them. I just wanted them to feel God reaching out to them with His wonderful message of acceptance and salvation through Jesus.

The third time I attempted to leave the token with this person was a success. They'd placed their keys on a table at a party and walked away. Stealthily, I deposited the token inside a circular indentation on an item attached to the keyring, into which the token fit perfectly. Proverbs 8:35 (TPT) says, "For the fountain of life pours into you every time that you find me, and this is the secret of growing in the delight and the favor of the Lord." God knew there was a void in this person's life that needed to be filled with Him. He led my friend out of the desert into a place where no believer is deserted.

> And because of him, when you who are not Jews heard the revelation of truth, you believed in the wonderful news of salvation. Now we have been stamped with the seal of the promised Holy Spirit. He is given to us like an engagement ring is given to a bride, as the first installment of what's coming! He is our hope-promise of a future inheritance which seals us until we have all of redemption's promises and experience complete freedom—all for the supreme glory and honor of God! (Ephesians 1:13-14 TPT).

> *Dear Lord Jesus, thank You for choosing me to reach the hurting and unsaved. Please give me the right words in the right moments to show someone how much You love them. Thank You for doing the same for me. In Your holy name I pray, amen.*

The Gift of Prophecy

If you've ever accurately predicted the outcome of an event or circumstance, you may have the gift of prophecy. You'll likely continue to predict things in the future and surprise people with accurate insight into their lives. Use your prophetic gift to edify, warn, heal and bless others, drawing them to God. You will likely even receive the occasional prophetic message yourself. Your vertical prayers and obedience allow God's power and knowledge to flow horizontally through you to others. Think of the vertical and horizontal pieces of the cross.

> And God has made all things new, and reconciled us to himself, and given us the ministry of reconciling others to God. In other words, it was through the Anointed One that God was shepherding the world, not even keeping records of their transgressions, and he has entrusted to us the ministry of opening the door of reconciliation to God. We are ambassadors of the Anointed One who carry the message of Christ to the world, as though God were tenderly pleading with them directly through our lips. So we tenderly plead with you on Christ's behalf, "Turn back to God and be reconciled to him" (2 Corinthians 5:18-20 TPT).

Once God has our trust and attention, He then calls us to share the gospel. Like Paul and many others, I've become a servant of this gospel, or a prophetess, by the gift of God's grace given me through His power. Why me? Paul explains that often outsiders are chosen to give the message of the cross—because they are *not* wise by human standards, influential, or of noble birth (1 Corinthians 1:26). So I share my "close encounters" and what God has blessed me with in order to glorify Him and draw people to Him.

My prophetic gifts include dreams, writing, and gift-giving. My dreams, stories, and gifts to others relate tangible evidence of God's beauty, protection, power, love, kindness, friendship, compassion, and forgiveness. While my writing is most often an external process that helps others understand God, my dreams help me understand and look forward to the future and protect me from harm. These prophetic glimpses, while wonderful and always welcome, are only a sneak peek of the great things to come for those who love Him (2 Corinthians 5:5).

> There has never been a generation that has been given the detailed understanding of this glorious and divine mystery until now. He kept it a secret until this generation. God is revealing it only now to his sacred apostles and prophets by the Holy Spirit. Here's the secret: The gospel of grace has made you, non-Jewish believers, into coheirs of his promise through your union with him. And you have now become members of his body—one with the Anointed One! (Ephesians 3:5-6 TPT).

> *Dear Lord Jesus, thank You for continual revelation and promises through dreams, visions, and epiphanies. Help me stay connected to You through prayer and obedience, and to use my gifts to help others and draw them to You. In Your holy name I pray, amen.*

430,000

God wants you, the recipient of His wonderful gifts, to use them in pursuit of the dreams and destiny He gives you. He knows you have a need to create and express yourself with them. He also knows who your endeavors will benefit. Your dreams and endeavors will flourish when you use your gifts to help others, furthering His kingdom. Drudgery is not part of the Father's plan for you and He longs to set you free from anything that would exploit or stifle your gifts.

> Now the length of time the Israelite people lived in Egypt was 430 years. At the end of the 430 years, to the very day, all the Lord's divisions left Egypt. Because the Lord kept vigil that night to bring them out of Egypt, on this night all the Israelites are to keep vigil to honor the Lord for the generations to come (Exodus 12:40-42 NIV).

Several years ago my husband shared a dream in which I'd inherited $430,000 from an unknown source. To consider this might actually be true one day is exciting in itself, but there is a deeper meaning. God often speaks to us using numbers. Biblically, the number 430 represents the time period between God's call on Abraham's life and the Exodus from Egypt. It represents freedom from bondage! Through a dream, God perfectly conveyed to me a promise of personal and financial freedom.

Not long afterward, I dreamt Nick received a specific monetary gift. Then in 2018 I had yet another specific dream in which we received a smaller gift, but one we desperately needed at the time. We received this smaller gift a few weeks later! And in 2019 we found out the bigger one would come to pass too. There seems to be a pattern in prophetic dreaming—the smaller the dream, the sooner it will come to pass.

Perhaps the bigger promises come to pass later because they require more preparation to receive.

> While he was still debating with himself about what to do, he fell asleep and had a supernatural dream. An angel from the Lord appeared to him in clear light and said, "Joseph, descendant of David, don't hesitate to take Mary into your home as your wife, because the power of the Holy Spirit has conceived a child in her womb. She will give birth to a son and you are to name him 'Savior,' for he is destined to give his life to save his people from their sins" (Matthew 1:20-21 TPT).

> *Dear Lord Jesus, thank You for deliverance, dreams of the future, promises that have come to pass, and inheritances along the way. Your sacrifice provides my way out of the wilderness and guarantees freedom for my children. In Your holy name I pray, amen.*

Writing

Everyone who has encountered Jesus will come away with different memories and a different interpretation of their experience. The more you share your stories about Him, the more light and hope will permeate the darkness to lift others up. If you choose to write, many of your readers will eagerly share with you how your writing has positively impacted them.

> And God-Enthroned spoke to me and said, "Consider this! I am making everything to be new and fresh. Write down at once all that I have told you, because each word is trustworthy and dependable" (Revelation 21:5 TPT).

Writing is my gift, as it's my most effective method of communication. As a little girl, I'd write lengthy notes to my parents and friends, and in grade school I'd write pieces that were publicly acknowledged by my teachers. I spent many long, dark days and nights in college writing about all sorts of empty topics that failed to encourage and bless me or my readers. I say those days were dark because the Lord's light had yet to fully dawn on me.

When I was thirty, after God revealed Himself to me and I began accumulating stories about Him, Nick encouraged me to begin writing creatively. I also told my prophetic aunt about the miraculous things I was experiencing. She said the Lord wanted me to write it all down; the dreams, visions, angelic encounters—all of it. So in 2014 I started a blog titled "Under God's Wings." It has been my destiny to write about the great love of our Lord Jesus.

Not long before I began compiling my blog posts for this book, I was chatting with our kids' prophetic babysitter, who didn't yet know much about my hobbies and talents. She said, "Do you like to write?" I responded yes and she went on to explain that she heard the Lord saying about me, "It's time to write." I was amazed at her insight and knew it was from God. She had confirmed what I'd been considering. I began writing this, my first book, within the week!

> He responded, "Every scholar of the Scriptures, who is instructed in the ways of heaven's kingdom realm, is like a wealthy home owner with his house filled with treasures both new and old. *And he knows how and when to bring them out to show others*" (Matthew 13:52 TPT).

> *Dear Lord Jesus, thank You for this powerful gift of (put your own spiritual gift here). I pray many others will find love and meaning in my work, prompting them to say a prayer, visit a church, or write down their own dream or vision from You! In Your holy name I pray, amen.*

Homebuilding

You may feel the Lord directing you to a specific ministry, perhaps to a specific group of people or to a specific geographic area. Just as He instructed Jonah to go to Nineveh, and the twelve disciples to the lost sheep of Israel (Matthew 10:6), He may be calling you to address a great need somewhere. He has qualified you for the job. And who knows, perhaps you've ascended to your royal position for such a time as this (Esther 4:14).

> Let me describe the one who truly follows me and does what I say. He is like a man who chooses the right place to build a house and then lays a deep and secure foundation. When the storms and floods rage against that house, it continues to stand strong and unshaken through the tempest, for it has been wisely built on the right foundation (Luke 6:47-48 TPT).

In my first dream about our destiny as homebuilders, Nick said to me, "I'm going to carry on my Dad's work, but I'm going to build the houses *because the labor is so cheap.*" We already understood the advantages of prefabricated construction methods and immediately realized the possibilities on a commercial scale. Further, Nick would be honoring his dad's homebuilding legacy as a provider of builder's insurance.

In late 2018, I received these instructions in a second dream, "Build affordable housing on the Beltline." This dream built upon the first, as we were instructed exactly where and what to build. In essence, the Atlanta Beltline is an oversized sidewalk loop that follows old railway lines and connects urban neighborhoods all over the city. It provides safety, fun, and connectivity for bikers, runners, families, and anyone who enjoys an alternative to urban vehicle travel. The popularity of the completed Beltline sections has resulted in skyrocketing property values and gentrification in the surrounding areas. This has been a boon for the city, but the trail leaves displaced rental residents in its wake in order to make way for new buyers from other areas.

In a third related dream, I was looking at a map of Atlanta. Glowing on the map was the roughly five-mile trail where the southernmost and final section of the Beltline will be built south of Interstate 20 over the next ten years. Written in beautiful cursive script along the glowing area was one word: "Beltline." This area is crime- and poverty-ridden, racially-homogeneous, and what some refer to as a "food desert," with very little to no healthy food available to purchase. This is where God wants us to start our business which will provide newly-built, high quality, efficient homes for existing rental residents to purchase at an affordable price.

> Is not this the kind of fasting I have chosen: to loose the chains of injustice and untie the cords of the yoke, to set the oppressed free and break every yoke? Is it not to share your food with the hungry and to provide the poor wanderer with shelter—when you see the naked, to clothe them, and not to turn away from your own flesh and blood? (Isaiah 58:6-7 NIV).

> *Dear Lord Jesus, thank You for showing us this incredible opportunity to minister to (put your own people group or geographic area here). Thank You for preparing us for such a time as this. Help us bring light and love into this area and help as many people as possible. In Your holy name I pray, amen.*

His Favor Lasts a Lifetime

Is there someone in your life you're at odds with? Does reconciliation with them seem impossible? Remember that with God, nothing is impossible. There is nothing you can say or do that God can't restore more beautifully than before it was broken. He's still there when the lights go out, when you're alone, and when all hope seems lost.

> The word from heaven will come to us with dazzling
> light to shine upon those who live in darkness, near
> death's dark shadow. And he will illuminate the path that
> leads to the way of peace (Luke 1:79 TPT).

One lonely night after an argument with my husband, I could only stare in bewilderment as I watched him leave me with all four kids in a tiny hotel room. That part of the evening is usually abuzz with activity, but this time there were just a few quietly-spoken questions, including, "Where did daddy go?" and, "Is he coming back?" I didn't know the answers, so I only said he'd gone for a ride and would probably be back soon.

I prayed and believed for a miracle that would restore our family. After I bathed, dressed, fed, calmed, and tucked in all four kids by myself, I sat alone in the pitch-black darkness. I remembered a recent headline in the news where some boys on a soccer team were trapped in a dark cave in Thailand. I felt strongly for them in their plight just then, and I prayed for them too. (Miraculously, all the boys and their coach were rescued.)

I stayed up late reading the Bible to search for clues about what was going to happen. Over and over, I found God's assurances telling me I'm His child and a good mother. There were also hints at some things I needed to change. If I wanted a lasting marriage, I was going to have to stop accusing Nick of wrongdoing and replace my suspicions and slander with love. I sent Nick a heartfelt apology and finally went to sleep.

In the morning, I checked my favorite daily Bible verse site and found a miraculous message. I felt sparks of hope and joy. Then, I discovered Nick had kindly left the car for us at the hotel the night before, so we were all reunited at home a couple of hours later. Although we didn't talk about our plans much past what we would do that day, I knew we would be okay, we would keep calm and carry on. The telling verse was Psalm 30:5 (TPT):

> I've learned that his anger lasts for a moment, but his loving favor lasts a lifetime! We may weep through the night, but at daybreak it will turn into shouts of ecstatic joy.

> *Dear Lord Jesus, thank You for forgiveness and assurances. Thank You for saving my family and holding us all together when calamity strikes. Help me not accuse my loved ones of wrongdoing, and to trust in Your perfect justice instead. In Your holy name I pray, amen.*

Israel's Future

God knows the plans He has for you, plans to prosper and not harm you, plans to give you hope and a future (Jeremiah 29:11 NIV). You may be in a place where none of that seems realistic. You may feel like your best days are way behind you. Understand that the promises God gives Israel throughout the Bible to purify, restore, and prosper her are promises for you too. You will be delivered from sin and made new to shine with the glory of the Lord. Jesus prophesied of Jerusalem:

> Many will be cut down by the sword or scattered as prisoners in many countries. And Jerusalem shall be trampled down by nations until the days of world empires come to an end (Luke 21:24 TPT).

The trampling Jesus refers to may have begun with the Roman Siege of Jerusalem in 70 AD. The historian Josephus claims that 1,100,000 people, the majority Jewish, were killed (fell by the edge of the sword) and 97,000 were captured and enslaved (led away captive). Many who survived and were not captured fled to other areas around the Mediterranean. These tragic events happened after Jesus was crucified by the Romans, although many Jews had believed Jesus would deliver them from Roman rule.

The two major, victorious events of the twentieth century in Israel's history were each commemorated by four total lunar eclipses in a row. A total lunar eclipse causes the moon to appear red in color, earning it the nickname of "blood moon." This pattern of "four blood moons," as detailed in Pastor John Hagee's book of the same name, occurred in 1949 and 1950 after Israel's rebirth as a nation in 1948, and again when Israel established control over Jerusalem in 1967 after the Six-Day War.[4]

---

4. "Eclipse Predictions by Fred Espenak, NASA GSFC Emeritus," NASA website, accessed December 12, 2019, https://eclipse.gsfc.nasa.gov/lunar.html.

As predicted by Hagee, the relatively recent tetrad of four back-to-back blood moons, occurring during the Jewish Holidays of Passover and Sukkot in 2014-2015, prefigured another major development in Jerusalem's restoration. In 2017, President Donald Trump announced the United States' recognition of Jerusalem as the capital of Israel and ordered the relocation of the U.S. Embassy in Israel from Tel Aviv to Jerusalem.[5]

It is widely believed the world empires will end at the Second Coming of the Lord, detailed in Revelation 19, after the gospel has been proclaimed to the whole world. Christ's return will complete the victory of Israel, and Isaiah's prophecy is evidence of Jerusalem's eventual restoration:

> For Zion's sake I will not keep silent, for Jerusalem's sake I will not remain quiet, till her vindication shines out like the dawn, her salvation like a blazing torch. The nations will see your vindication, and all kings your glory; you will be called by a new name that the mouth of the Lord will bestow. You will be a crown of splendor in the Lord's hand, a royal diadem in the hand of your God. No longer will they call you Deserted, or name your land Desolate. But you will be called Hephzibah, and your land Beulah; for the Lord will take delight in you, and your land will be married. As a young man marries a young woman, so will your Builder marry you; as a bridegroom rejoices over his bride, so will your God rejoice over you (Isaiah 62:1-5 NIV).

> *Dear Lord Jesus, thank You for signs and wonders in the sky confirming the events that are of importance to You and Your children. Help me to always remember Israel as the apple of Your eye, and to pray for her restoration. In Your holy name I pray, amen.*

---

5. "Statement by President Trump on Jerusalem," The White House website, December 6, 2017, accessed October 11, 2019, https://www.whitehouse.gov/briefings-statements/statement-president-trump-jerusalem/

Three Sisters to Meet

If you've got siblings, you know how wonderful and challenging it is to grow up with other children. You probably helped each other learn, protected each other from harm, and kept each other entertained. Most importantly, you always had a friend! Please don't let troubled sibling relationships or worries prevent you from having multiple children. God can heal your sibling relationships and bless your children's.

> How truly wonderful and delightful to see brothers and sisters living together in sweet unity! (Psalm 133:1 TPT).

> Sweet friendships refresh the soul and awaken our hearts with joy, for good friends are like the anointing oil that yields the fragrant incense of God's presence (Proverbs 27:9 TPT).

Several years ago, my mother's sister shared with me a dream she'd had about me. In it, she saw three young women about my age sitting at a table. They spoke to her and claimed to be my sisters living in heaven. My aunt believes these women are actually my sisters who were never born because my mother had a few troubled pregnancies. God was so kind to give me this message, as I'd often wondered why I didn't have siblings.

My mother hasn't shared with me the details regarding her three other pregnancies. She may have miscarried, or she may have, unfortunately, decided she couldn't support four children. Based on what God chose to include in the dream, what happened in the past isn't what matters. He gave me a glimpse of my sisters so I can look forward to a beautiful future in heaven with them.

It may be no coincidence that I happened to be writing on this topic (pre-set in my calendar) on our nation's first annual Day of Mourning. It has been established by pro-life activists as a day to gather, pray, and worship in solidarity with the pre-born. I'm so grateful I never had to consider abortion, as my children are truly my joy and purpose. Prior to having them, I asked the Lord for things amiss. Once I realized I wanted children and began praying for this, He began blessing us with one after the other!

Children born to a young couple will one day rise to protect and provide for their parents. Happy will be the couple who has many of them. A household full of children will not bring shame on your name but victory when you face your enemies, for your offspring will have influence and honor to prevail on your behalf! (Psalm 127:4-5 TPT).

Dear Lord Jesus, thank You for blessing our family with our wonderful children. Please let them follow after You all of their days, stay in Your Word, and always shine bright for You. I also thank You that all the innocent lives taken during abortion are resting in peace with You. I pray their would-be friends and family will repent, be forgiven, and be given another chance to receive your blessings. I also ask that our nation would repent of its evil practice of abortion, and that You would heal and restore our nation from the infant holocaust. In Your holy name I pray, amen.

Pregnant with Promise

Are there dreams and ideas you carry around, not sure when or how to go about acting on them? Perhaps you started a project or business a while ago, only to watch it get pushed to the back burner. God plants these seeds of promise in everyone. He often plants them early in life so we can watch them unfold slowly before us. Do not worry if you feel like your promise has been forgotten. He is preparing you to receive, in His timing, His mandate for action and His rewards for obedience.

> Mary rode into Bethlehem carrying a promise, the promise of a new thing, the promise of a new hope, the promise of expectation, the promise of a new life, the promise of a harvest. You are going to run with joy in your field of supernatural harvest! This is your season of Great Expectation.[6]

One morning when I was just a couple of months pregnant with Evelyn, I stumbled upon an online article by Dana Jarvis titled, "Pregnant with Promise!" It spoke right to me, illuminating that I'd withstood pain and the enemy's persecution and was finally entering into a birthing season. I was waiting on promises, including two additional babes, Evelyn and Nick Jr. It was a season of hope, expectation, pushing, knocking on heaven's doors, and remembering God's answered prayers!

At that point, I hadn't told anyone of my pregnancy, with the exception of Nick and my mom. I was beyond thrilled but didn't want to risk telling anyone else, because the pregnancy wasn't very far along. The babysitter who was working with us, who was also a student at Bethel Atlanta at the

6. "God Said 'Yes,'" by Dana Jarvis, The Elijah List Facebook page, Posted April 21, 2016, used by permission of Elijah List Publications, Inc., accessed October 11, 2019, https://www.facebook.com/TheElijahList/photos/a.10151826924153989/10154780923303989.

time, is prophetic. She arrived at our house later the same morning I read the article. Miraculously, she'd heard the Lord say that I was "pregnant with promise." She believed I would give birth to some sort of faith-based, creative project or ministry. She didn't know I was literally pregnant until I told her. She and I were amazed at how accurate she'd been, and doubly amazed about how the article had foreshadowed her prophecy. Her word of knowledge served as confirmation that I was not only carrying a beautiful person and some amazing dreams, but also that they would eventually come to fruition: "So also will be the word that I speak; it does not return to me unfulfilled. My word performed my purpose and fulfills the mission I sent it out to accomplish" (Isaiah 55:11 TPT).

This book and our forthcoming homebuilding business are projects God has been cultivating in us since 2014, maybe even before. Back then I couldn't have guessed what He had planned for us over the next decade. We had three more wonderful children, got completely out of debt *three times*, were delivered from sin and bondage, forgave and were forgiven, dreamed dreams, inherited a goldmine of knowledge regarding the gospel, and have made significant progress toward seeing our book and business "babies" realized. We are putting our backgrounds and educations to their best creative, kingdom-inspired uses. And I'm sure there are wonders and surprises that are still in store for us!

> This is why the Scriptures say: Things never discovered or heard of before, things beyond our ability to imagine— these are the many things God has in store for all his lovers (1 Corinthians 2:9 TPT).

> *Dear Lord Jesus, thank You for dreams and promises that have already come to fruition, and for those that are still promises to come. Thank You for prophecy and encouragement along the way. Help me be patient during the waiting and preparation. In Your holy name I pray, amen.*

Number Five

Joanna Gaines announced her fifth pregnancy when she was forty years old. This news got me excited, hopeful, and amazed at God's goodness, even during mid-life. You might be discouraged if you believe your best years are behind you. But God will surprise you later in life with new people, projects, and adventures. Your life in five years may be unrecognizable—in a wonderful way! You may even have a hunch about what is coming already. He plants seeds in our hearts to plan for and look forward to. If you're experiencing a quiet season, He may be giving you time to enjoy what He's already blessed you with while preparing you for the new that's to come.

> Because you received a double dose of shame and dishonor, you will inherit a double portion of endless joy and everlasting bliss! (Isaiah 61:7 TPT).

When I prayed for Evelyn, I only asked for one little girl. It never occurred to me to ask for two. Just a few months prior to becoming pregnant with her in 2016, I received a word clearly from the Lord regarding our family. I was reading an article and came across the words, *your girls*. At that moment I felt strongly that He was clearly highlighting these words to me as a promise for the future. At the time I was thrilled and in disbelief because we had two little boys. I'd come from a small family, having no siblings. To think I might one day have four children was almost too good to dream.

After we had Evelyn, I thought to myself, "We'll have one more little girl and our family will be complete!" Imagine my confusion ten weeks into my fourth pregnancy when our midwife delivered the news that we'd soon bring a third little boy into the world. God promised we'd have another girl. How could He be wrong? It slowly dawned on me He wasn't wrong—we would have another little girl. She would be number five! First, I believe we will enjoy a good three to four years of transition, rest, and adventures as we begin homeschooling Jackson and Charlie, and as Evy and Baby Nick mature into school-age.

As I sat in my vehicle writing the first part of this entry, titled Number Five, I looked out the windshield at the office building across the street. I was wondering again if I'd actually understood God correctly. Did I really believe He'd bless us with a fifth child sometime in the future? As I pondered, my gaze landed on a giant metal sign that said *"#5"* attached to the office building I'd been looking at. In that moment, I knew God was answering my question. He showed us years ago that He would eventually send a double pink blessing, and He loves to remind me occasionally.

> For this is the hope of our salvation. But hope means that we must trust and wait for what is still unseen. For why would we need to hope for something we already have? So because our hope is set on what is yet to be seen, we patiently keep on waiting for its fulfillment. And in a similar way, the Holy Spirit takes hold of us in our human frailty to empower us in our weakness. For example, at times we don't even know how to pray, or know the best things to ask for. But the Holy Spirit rises up within us to super-intercede on our behalf, pleading to God with emotional sighs too deep for words (Romans 8:24-26 TPT).

Dear Lord Jesus, thank You for promising more than I could ask for. Help me to wait patiently, joyfully, and expectantly for Your double blessing. You are the one who gives in good measure, pressed down, shaken together, and running over. In Your holy name I pray, amen.

Dream Home

Do you long for a place you've never been? Maybe you don't feel settled or satisfied where you are. You just know that even in the comfort of your house, you don't feel at home. I've heard it said that Jesus planted heaven in our hearts. We are temporary inhabitants of a strange world where pain and loss abound, and we long for our eternal, blissful home with the Lord. We weren't born to achieve comfort or perfection on earth, but to first do the Lord's work of helping others.

> Don't worry or surrender to your fear. For you've believed in God, now trust and believe in me also. My Father's house has many dwelling places. If it were otherwise, I would tell you plainly, because I go to prepare a place for you to rest. (John 14:1-2 TPT).

When I was writing this book, we were renting a home. The rental was big enough for our children to each have their own bedroom, it was conveniently located about ten minutes from work, local attractions, and shopping, and was less expensive than our previous mortgage. It was a great place to rest and transition into all God has for us in terms of dream realization, healing, homeschooling, and generally settling into a new freedom Nick and I have never experienced before. Renting was fine for a season or two, but soon we will be happy homeowners.

Our next home will be brand new, built by us and for us. I believe God's preparing us now as to how and what to buy. He's guiding us first to realize my literal dream to build affordable, prefab homes for others. Through this endeavor we will earn the skills, confidence, and money needed to build a home for our six-to-seven-person family. It is not

His will for his children to go into debt (Romans 13:8) or to undertake something major without sufficient wisdom and understanding.

We are to build new two-to-three-bedroom homes for others in order to make the additional money needed to build our own. If we bought our house first, we would have to take out a jumbo loan with nothing leftover to start building for others. Putting others first is biblical and will benefit us in the long run, so it's a win-win all around. We have our dreams of exactly what and where to build, and, according to the US Census, Atlanta gets thirty-six new residents every day![7]

Once we've helped several other families buy an affordable new home and make a great investment, we will have enough profit to build our own home without a loan. Mortgage debt is bondage, regardless of how many people say it's "good debt." There is no freedom in the bondage of debt. Jesus came to set us free so we can pursue more of Him with no tangled, hard-to-exit commitments. It's my dream to build our next home new, own it free of debt, and use it to continually love others.

> This is what the Lord Almighty says: "Give careful thought to your ways. Go up into the mountains and bring down timber and build my house, so that I may take pleasure in it and be honored," says the Lord. "You expected much, but see, it turned out to be little. What you brought home, I blew away. Why?" declares the Lord Almighty. "Because of my house, which remains a ruin, while each of you is busy with your own house" (Haggai 1:7-9 NIV).

> Don't owe anything to anyone, except your outstanding debt to continually love one another, for the one who learns to love has fulfilled every requirement of the law (Romans 13:8 TPT).

---

7. "U.S. Census: Atlanta sees 36 new residents every day," Eric Mandel, Atlanta Business Chronicle, posted May 29, 2018, accessed October 11, 2019, https://www.bizjournals.com/atlanta/news/2018/05/29/u-s-census-atlanta-sees-36-new-residents-every-day.html.

Dear Lord Jesus, thank You for showing me how to love others before myself. Help me be selfless, chasing after your kingdom first, and to remember everything else will be added to me. Thank You for placing heaven in my heart. In Your holy name I pray, amen.

Part 4:

Commission

Just as the Father has sent me, I'm now sending you.

John 20:21 (TPT)

Dark Places

Sharing the gospel can be intimidating, especially if you're speaking with an unbeliever or someone who's hostile to your message. Unless you have a background in apologetics, you're not expected to persuade anyone to accept Christ using lengthy arguments or theological research. Instead, the world will see Him in your words, actions, and demeanor. Just be yourself, employ kindness, and help them understand that He loves them even more than you do. You'll plant a tiny seed within their heart that God will later cultivate.

> Walk in the wisdom of God as you live before the unbelievers, and make it your duty to make him known. Let every word you speak be drenched with grace and tempered with truth and clarity. For then you will be prepared to give a respectful answer to anyone who asks about your faith (Colossians 4:5-6 TPT).

I once participated in Bethel School's ministry outreach in Atlanta's Five Points neighborhood. Students would gather to pray and then disperse, typically in pairs, to reach out to strangers in need of prayer and encouragement. I was paired with another young woman and we wandered around the shops while she talked to people she knew from previous days of outreach. Although we very much enjoyed the nice weather and light conversation with friendly folks, we also wanted to meet new people and uphold the instructions for ministry outlined above in Colossians 4:5-6.

We'd been exploring the neighborhood for about a half-hour when she asked if there was any place in particular I felt we should go. I'd been told about a coffee shop operated by people practicing witchcraft, so I mentioned it.

For some reason, my first inclination in most situations is to embark on the most challenging mission—qualified or not. One time I found myself at the top of a black diamond ski slope because the other slopes were just a bit boring and crowded. After barely making it down the black diamond slope with my life, I then opted for the slopes labeled with prettier colors.

This particular day, my new friend replied, "Oh yeah, I've been in there before. They have good coffee. You wanna go?" I couldn't argue with that. Jesus wasn't telling me not to go, and my new super laid-back hipster friend said the coffee was good. So we went.

There was no question as to which shop it was. The stuff posted on the windows was disturbing, to say the least. I'd never seen such a creepy place and didn't want to go in. I stopped outside the door, waiting for Jesus to give me a red or green light. I didn't hear Him, but I've learned that He will most definitely speak up when danger is imminent. We'd been outside debating a few moments when a group of several happy young adults walked right in, apparently excited about getting coffee. They didn't seem concerned, so why should we be? I took that as a good sign and said, "Okay, let's go."

We entered, the door closed behind us, and I was instantly overcome with grief. There was nowhere to rest my eyes; it was all awful. Blasphemous and disturbing objects, artwork, signage, and decorations were everywhere. The creepiest of techno music was playing. I walked up to the counter to order a beverage. By that time a line had formed at the counter and tears had formed in my eyes.

When I made eye contact with the young lady behind the counter, my grief multiplied. She looked miserable. There wasn't a trace of happiness on her face or in her voice, and her eyes had a glassy lifelessness about them. I'm not positive, but I think I saw her wipe away a tear too. The people in line were glancing at me, probably wondering why I'd walked in and broken into tears. When it was my turn to order, I could barely speak. Her eyes flicked from mine to the cross necklace I was wearing and then away. She wouldn't maintain eye contact. I didn't feel hostility from her, just annoyance.

After she'd given me the check and my drink, I said, "Jesus loves you." This really didn't appear to go over well. Without responding, she walked to the other end of the bar where some friends were sitting, to whom she posed the question, "Hey guys, does Jesus love me?" I would very much like to forget what one of the guys said about Him. As I took a seat near their group, the two on either side of me got up and left, the mouthy fellow headed toward the door without making eye contact, and the lady behind the counter headed back toward the cash register. It was definitely not happy hour. The cashier wished me a good day when we left, prompting our group of ministry friends to pray over me for a complete spiritual cleansing.

I took comfort back home later that evening from 1 Peter 4:14 (TPT): "If you are insulted because of the name of Christ, you are greatly blessed, because the Spirit of glory and power, who is the Spirit of God, rests upon you." Jesus confirmed that we'd done the right thing by visiting the coffee shop for the purpose of loving this lady in His name. Although shaken and completely drained of energy from the fifteen minutes we spent inside the shop, I felt that He had reached this lady through my clumsy attempt to connect, letting her know that He loves her and wants her back. I decided I would visit her again one day, for Hebrews 13:3 (TPT) says, "Identify with those who are in prison as though you were there suffering with them, and those who are mistreated as if you could feel their pain."

Just a couple of months later, my husband and son and I visited a bakery not too far from the creepy coffee shop. To my delight and surprise, the barista from that terrible shop was now working at the happy bakery. Her friendly demeanor was completely different from our first encounter. I gave her a new cross necklace I just happened to have in my bag, and she gave me a complimentary coffee. According to her sister, who also worked at the bakery, my new friend was trying to turn her life around and leave the darkness behind. Only God could do this wonderful work!

> Where could I go from your Spirit? Where could I run and
> hide from your face? If I go up to heaven, you're there! If

I go down to the realm of the dead, you're there too! If I fly with wings into the shining dawn, you're there! If I fly into the radiant sunset, you're there waiting! Wherever I go, your hand will guide me; your strength will empower me. It's impossible to disappear from you, or to ask the darkness to hide me, for your presence is everywhere, bringing light into my night. (Psalm 139:7-11 TPT).

Dear Lord Jesus, thank You for being with me in dark places and dangerous circumstances, among unbelievers and even those who are hostile. Help me always speak with grace tempered with truth and clarity so You will always be on display. Help me to not be afraid or overcome. In Your holy name I pray, amen.

Eat with the Sick

Have you ever been invited to a wedding, dinner party, reception, or banquet for a group that you just weren't quite sure about? Perhaps their views were extremely liberal and quite different from yours. Maybe they're just a "rough crowd" and considered somewhat socially unacceptable. Understand that you don't have to agree with them or engage in their business or interests in order to minister to them. Just by accepting their invitation and joining them for a couple of hours over a meal or meeting, you're not subscribing to their point of view. You will, however, honor them and gain their attentive ear for a chance to tell them about our Lord and Savior. If they are celebrating or engaging in something you don't agree with, simply step out for a few moments to wait kindly and quietly for your opportunity to return and lovingly point them toward Jesus.

> Later, Jesus and his disciples went to have a meal with Levi. Among the guests in Levi's home were many tax collectors and notable sinners sharing a meal with Jesus, for there were many kinds of people who followed him. But when the religious scholars and the Pharisees found out that Jesus was keeping company and dining with sinners and tax collectors, they were indignant. So they approached Jesus' disciples and said to them, "Why is it that someone like Jesus defiles himself by eating with sinners and tax collectors?" But when Jesus overheard their complaint, he said to them, "Who goes to the doctor for a cure? Those who are well or those who are sick? I have not come to call the 'righteous,' but to call those who are sinners and bring them to repentance" (Mark 2:15-17 TPT).

Once at a restaurant with Nick and Jackson during a vacation in Fort Lauderdale I noticed a flag indicator that the restaurant was welcoming of people in relationships which are outlined in the Bible as forbidden. As we debated on whether the three of us would be welcome there and if it would be a safe family environment, God reminded me of a Bible verse I had read recently in Mark 2:13-17. The Pharisees had questioned Jesus' decision to eat with the "tax collectors and sinners" who followed Him. The Pharisees used the word "sinners" to refer to any people not obeying all the commandments and rules outlined in the Old Testament. These rules number more than 1500—and are so difficult to obey that Jesus had to die on the cross to fulfill the rules and pay for our sins. Jesus replied to the Pharisees that only the sick need a doctor, and that He had come to call sinners to repentance. He is here to help everyone, although each person has a different struggle.

Even though the restaurant owners were evidently proud of a lifestyle that God does not condone, choosing to go elsewhere for dinner would not make us more righteous in His eyes. Righteousness does not come by judging oneself against others, by refusing to eat at certain places, or by boycotting certain businesses. We all fall short of God's standards, so to be saved we must choose to accept, follow, obey, and listen to Jesus, repenting and asking forgiveness daily. We all need Him. However, Jesus' sacrifice must not be used as a license to do whatever we please. Although we will continue to make mistakes as long as we live, He knows our heart and sees our genuine desire to be obedient.

We entered the restaurant and were given a couple of puzzled looks as we were greeted and seated. Fortunately (and God already knew this) Jackson encountered nothing inside that was inappropriate for a toddler to see. The reviews were right—the food was great and the owner kind. Before we left, God urged me to leave the book I was reading titled *Seeing and Savoring Jesus Christ*. I left it on the table with a note of appreciation for the dining experience. On the way out, I noticed a cross on the wall immediately inside the main entrance. It appeared to be displayed out of respect, and I left feeling glad for

God's continual presence and guidance even in times of uncertainty. God later led me to Joshua 1:9 which confirms His companionship and protection in all situations:

> Have I not commanded you? Be strong and courageous. Do not be afraid; do not be discouraged, for the Lord your God will be with you wherever you go (Joshua 1:9 NIV).

Dear Lord Jesus, thank You for courage and light in dark places. I won't fear the enemy in there, and I will trust that You walk with me anywhere I venture to spread the good news of Your unconditional love. In Your holy name I pray, amen.

Travel Lightly

Is there someone you can forgive today? Ask God to help you let go of any anxiety, resentment, or misconceptions you may still have when you think about them. Then ask Him to bless them so they will know His love and kindness. Forgive the people who hurt you, let go of the past, and believe God's promises for your future.

> But instead be kind and affectionate toward one another. Has God graciously forgiven you? Then graciously forgive one another in the depths of Christ's love (Ephesians 4:32 TPT).

Whenever we pack in preparation to move to a different house, we start with our books, wedding dishes, stemware, and photo frames. Afterward, the house feels tidy. I don't miss these items for a while because we don't use them much, with the exception of the children's books. Most of my favorite books and photos are stored online. Part of me feels like it's wasted effort to continue the cycle of packing and unpacking them with each move. After all, they have been traveling with us from house to house since 2005, only to sit mostly unused on a shelf in the new home once unpacked.

In my heart I know it's not wasteful or ungrateful to donate or dispose of items I haven't used in a while because they're outdated or no longer fit. However, I'm so attached to some useless items that the thought of parting with them causes feelings of guilt. The truth is, clearing out the old may take us on a trip down memory lane, but it shouldn't be a guilt trip. Perhaps it's the reminder of how much I spent, or of the generosity of the person who gifted it to me, or even the fear of not having it in the future that keeps me from "tossing" an item when it's time.

Jesus instructed his disciples to "take only your staff and the sandals on your feet—no bread, no knapsack, no extra garment, and no money" (Mark 6:8-9 TPT). He wanted them to not only trust Him completely for provision, but also to walk unhindered in His freedom. If we are too attached to remnants of our past or fear not having enough on the journey, it will take longer to prepare when God is ready to take us on a different adventure or gift us with something new. Imagine if He said, "Go!" and we could simply pack a bag of essentials and hop in the car with our loved ones. How much more exciting, free, and easy would that be than spending an overwhelming month packing countless boxes of wedding dishes, stemware, and paperback novels?

Just as material baggage hinders transition and advancement, unpleasant memories affect the mind in the same way, cluttering it up with post-traumatic stress, regret, and unforgiveness. Continually looking backward into the past with unhealed wounds will delay us from reaching the abundant, new life God has planned for us— because our thoughts affect behavior and relationships.

> As for us, we have all of these great witnesses who encircle us like clouds. So we must let go of every wound that has pierced us and the sin we so easily fall into. Then we will be able to run life's marathon race with passion and determination, for the path has been already marked out before us (Hebrews 12:1 TPT).

> I don't depend on my own strength to accomplish this; however I do have one compelling focus: I forget all of the past as I fasten my heart to the future instead. I run straight for the divine invitation of reaching the heavenly goal and gaining the victory-prize through the anointing of Jesus (Philippians 3:13-14 TPT).

> *Dear Lord Jesus, thank You for pioneering seasons of following the path You've set before me. Thank You for*

forgiving me of all my mistakes and unbelief. Help me to forgive others as You've done for me. And help me to move forward in Your freedom without physical and spiritual baggage. In Your name I pray, amen.

God is Love

Jesus makes it clear you can expect to receive joy and blessing when you obey His command to love. Although the opportunities to literally lay down one's life for another may be few and far between, there are studies showing that "laying down" your precious resources for others makes everyone happy. At TEDxCambridge, Michael Norton shares research on how money can, indeed, buy happiness—when you spend it on others.[8]

> So this is my command: Love each other deeply, as much as I have loved you. For the greatest love of all is a love that sacrifices all. And this great love is demonstrated when a person sacrifices his life for his friends (John 15:12-13 TPT).

There is one command from Jesus that is so simple and intuitive that anyone can do it. It requires no skill, no education, little to no resources, no great effort, and not even a strong belief in the unseen. It is simply to love one another. Babies love people from birth, yet they haven't been told to do so. They instinctively and immediately want to be held and nurtured by their parents, which is an expression of love. Babies do naturally what kids and adults sometimes find difficult.

We must also choose to follow the Ten Commandments out of love for others, including Jesus. It's impossible to break one without hurting Him or someone else. Keeping them also ensures our own freedom and well-being of our mind and body, which only a loving God would desire for His children. These are the Ten Commandments, found in Exodus 20 (NIV):

---

8. "How to Buy Happiness," Michael Norton, video content from Ted posted November 2011, accessed October 11, 2019, https://www.ted.com/talks/michael_norton_how_to_buy_happiness?utm_campaign=tedspread&utm_medium=referral&utm_source=tedcomshare

1. You shall have no other gods before me.

2. You shall not make for yourself an image in the form of anything in heaven above or on the earth beneath or in the waters below. You shall not bow down to them or worship them.

3. You shall not misuse the name of the Lord your God, for the Lord will not hold anyone guiltless who misuses his name.

4. Remember the Sabbath day by keeping it holy. Six days you shall labor and do all your work, but the seventh day is a sabbath to the Lord your God.

5. Honor your father and your mother, so that you may live long in the land the Lord your God is giving you.

6. You shall not murder.

7. You shall not commit adultery.

8. You shall not steal.

9. You shall not give false testimony against your neighbor.

10. You shall not covet your neighbor's house. You shall not covet your neighbor's wife, or his male or female servant, his ox or donkey, or anything that belongs to your neighbor.

Beyond the Big Ten, we also receive personal commands and requests from Jesus: "The heart of the wise will easily accept instruction" (Proverbs 10:8 TPT). He asks for simple acts of love, generosity, and kindness toward others that produce the fruit He talks about in John 15. No one but Jesus is perfect, but we can always get one thing right—love others as He loves us. By loving others, we display the forgiveness and love Jesus has for them and gain their trust. Once they understand that they're loved without judgment, they'll be more likely to accept Him as their Lord and Savior.

> Hatred keeps old quarrels alive, but love draws a veil over every insult and finds a way to make sin disappear (Proverbs 10:12 TPT).

Dear Lord Jesus, thank You for making clear exactly what I must do to live a peaceful, joy-filled life of blessing. Help me to always love others and love You, never forgetting Your commands. I want my words and actions to attract people to You. In Your holy name I pray, amen.

Power of the Cross

Do you remember the first time someone explained to you who God is? Was it difficult to comprehend His existence, death, and resurrection? There is so much to know about Him, but the best news is that He loves you enough to reconcile you to Himself through Jesus' death on the cross (Colossians 1:20). Further, He has entrusted you with the power of the gospel to help save, heal, and deliver others, just as He has done for you!

> But I promise you this—the Holy Spirit will come upon you and you will be filled with power. And you will be my messengers to Jerusalem, throughout Judea, the distant provinces—even to the remotest places on earth! (Acts 1:8 TPT).

God used the cross in an immediate way to save our son Jackson as a baby. When he was born, he was gifted a small ceramic cross that was inscribed with "Jesus Loves Me." We adhered it lightly to the center mullion of the window above Jackson's crib. One day when he was just learning to stand, I put him in his crib for a nap and went downstairs to work. Several minutes later I heard something crash loudly to the floor. I hurried up to his room to find him playing with the long cords that control the window shades. In the process he'd knocked the cross off the window.

We had left his crib much too close to the window where he could reach the cords—which is a strangling hazard to babies. God used the cross to alert me to this dangerous situation before it was too late. He goes to great lengths to protect His flock, especially the smallest and most helpless. The cross has the power to save both our lives and our souls.

I am the Good Shepherd who lays down my life as a sacrifice for the sheep.... I give to them the gift of eternal life and they will never be lost and no one has the power to snatch them out of my hands (John 10:11, 28 TPT).

Dear Lord Jesus, thank You for making me right with God. Because of Your resurrection, I am righteous in my Father's eyes and will never know His wrath. Thank You for protecting me and my loved ones, and reminding me of the mighty power of the cross. I want to learn more about You every day. In Your holy name I pray, amen.

Sharing is Caring

Even if you're not Billy Graham, your kind words and actions can speak volumes about our Lord and Savior to other people. Maybe you have a speech impediment like Moses (Exodus 4:10), or simply fear talking to others about your beliefs. Don't be discouraged. As long as you have a heart of love, you can share the gospel effectively. God promises to help you speak and to teach you what to say if you will just go! (Exodus 4:12)

> For while I was with you I was determined to be consumed with one topic—Jesus, the crucified Messiah.
> (1 Corinthians 2:2 TPT).

We sat silently staring out at the putting green and driving range. Apparently, there was confusion among the event organizers regarding the logistics of the putting contest, even though the rules were simple: A hole-in-one wins. For about an hour I'd been chatting with a young college student about his degree program, how we'd each come to volunteer at the golf tournament, the beautiful weather, etc. The small talk eventually ran out, and there we sat together in a golf cart with nothing left to say. The putting contest we were supposed to oversee had been postponed until 1:30, and our shift would soon be over. So far, I'd been unproductive at the event other than to catch a few rays of sun.

Sitting there in silence, I realized God's hand had brought us together so I could tell him about Jesus. So I told him about a movie I had just watched about a college student who proves that God is real to his professor. I gave a synopsis of the movie, and he shared that he's Muslim and pointed out that Islam and Christianity have similarities. When he asked for an explanation of the Holy Trinity, I thought of the triangle I'd seen in the sky on the way to the golf course and responded that God is one being with three distinct but equal elements: Father God in heaven, Jesus who lived and died as a person for our sins, and Holy Spirit who lives within those who accept Jesus as Lord and Savior, transforming them from the inside out. The result is a relationship with Jesus, rather than a life lived to follow the rules.

Finally, I shared with him the testimony of a man who converted to Christianity from Islam after receiving dreams and visions from the Lord. By 1:30, there had been no putting contest for us to oversee, but I left feeling grateful for such a happy and relaxing opportunity to share the gospel. Because Jesus is kind, His assignments are enjoyable.

> For all that I require of you will be pleasant and easy to bear (Matthew 11:30 TPT).

> *Dear Lord Jesus, thank You for an easy yoke and a light burden. Thank You also for Your prompts and reminders when I have the opportunity to tell someone about You. Like Moses and Paul, I will rely on Your power to convey Your message of love and hope. If I plant the seed in a stranger's heart, You will take care of it. In Your holy name I pray, amen.*

Holy Spirit Counsel

The next time you open your Bible, take a moment before you start reading to ask God for insight into the text. As you're reading, what appears on the surface to be an old story will suddenly come to life! It will become your story too. You are not meant to walk through your storms and celebrations alone. Read the Bible to find His instruction and wisdom regarding your personal challenges and victories. He was with us on earth and now, through His Word and Spirit, God says, "Never forget that I am with you every day, even to the completion of this age." (Matthew 28:20 TPT)

> The secret things belong to the Lord our God, but the things revealed belong to us and to our children forever, that we may follow all the words of this law (Deuteronomy 29:29 NIV).

> But God now unveils these profound realities to us by the Spirit. Yes, he has revealed to us his inmost heart and deepest mysteries through the Holy Spirit, who constantly explores all things (1 Corinthians 2:10 TPT).

One weekend in February of 2014, I had the privilege of attending a church service in Tyrone, Georgia, led by guest speaker Bill Johnson of Bethel Redding in California. He was visiting Bethel Atlanta, a church plant southwest of the city. Bill's ministry is known to welcome and delight in the presence of the Holy Spirit, and attendees report regular occurrences of the Spirit's physical manifestation through signs and healings.

Prior to hearing Bill speak, I'd heard of really cool things happening at his services, like gold dust falling from the sky and glory clouds appearing near the ceiling. He and his ministry team are known for miraculous healings by God's power, including metal implants disappearing, missing body parts regenerating, the blind seeing, and the lame walking.

That Saturday night as he was wrapping up his message, people in the audience began pointing at something just above and in front of where Bill was standing on stage. I looked up to see they were pointing to a bright green feather that had literally appeared out of nowhere. It was easy to see from across the room because of its vivid color. We all gasped in unison as it floated over heads toward the back of the room.

I interpret feathers to mean God's presence and protection, and Bill noted that green also symbolizes financial blessing. After the service I heard reports that the green feather made its way to someone in the audience who received physical healing that evening. I must have shared that story with everyone I know who would listen. It was amazing!

Bill encourages everyone to pursue a deeply personal relationship with Jesus for many reasons, one being that God will reveal His mysteries to those who rely on the Holy Spirit to enhance their understanding of Him and His Word. What God chooses to reveal may not be clearly identified in Scripture. The revelation He shares with you personally may provide new insight to something in Scripture, or He may encourage you to look something up in Scripture. We have God's stated and official words in the Bible, but He also promises to interact with us so our learning becomes personal and relevant to our experiences.

> I hear the Lord saying, "I will stay close to you, instructing and guiding you along the pathway for your life. I will advise you along the way and lead you forth with my eyes as your guide. So don't make it difficult; don't be stubborn when I take you where you've not been before. Don't make me tug you and pull you along. Just come with me!" (Psalm 32:8-9 TPT).

> *Dear Lord Jesus, thank You for revealing mysteries and hidden meanings. Thank You for beautiful displays of Your power and miraculous healings. Please give me the confidence and opportunities to pray for others' healing and circumstances. In Your holy name I pray, amen.*

Teachers

If you're like me, you're a lifelong learner, constantly thirsting for knowledge and direction. There is so much to learn about God and the kingdom of heaven, but where should you go for biblically-based instruction on these seemingly-infinite topics? You'll know a genuine teacher by their fruit. Is it sweet or rotten? Good fruit isn't found on a thorn bush or tumbleweed. (Matthew 7:15-20) Study the results of their actions and the work of their ministries. Are they helping the poor and needy, the orphans and widows? Do they defend the defenseless? Are they a voice for the voiceless? (Proverbs 31:8-9) If the answer is yes, you've found a true teacher you can trust.

> Your extravagant kindness to me makes me want to follow your words even more! Teach me how to make good decisions, and give me revelation-light, for I believe in your commands. Before I was humbled I used to always wander astray, but now I see the wisdom of your words. Everything you do is beautiful, flowing from your goodness; teach me the power of your wonderful words! (Psalm 119:65-68 TPT).

Regular church attendance is the easiest and most cost-effective way to learn more about God and His Word. It's not necessary to go every week or even to the same church to learn, because a good sermon can stand alone, even if it's part of a series. Many church services are available online as either a live stream or an archive download. The preachers I love use a combination of Scripture, humor, testimony, and prayer to convey spiritual wisdom and truth. I love Joel Osteen for his positivity and messages of hope and prosperity. I love all of the teachers at Bethel Redding and Bethel Atlanta for their messages of God's unconditional love and unlimited healing power.

Speaking events, conferences, and workshops are also great opportunities to hear from good teachers and get their books. I loved attending Bethel Atlanta's Sunday service, and sometimes even night classes as a guest in their school of ministry, when we lived nearby. Bethel hosts many guest speakers with fresh and inspiring messages— like Shawn Bolz. He is an amazingly accurate prophet who frequently speaks directly to people in the audience using information he receives from God on the spot.

On the one occasion I heard Shawn speak, he asked if there was someone in the audience who does gymnastics, and he listed a couple of other identifying activities. Several people in the audience suggested he call a particular young woman, the ministry school's worship leader, who is also one of our family's favorite babysitters. He called her from stage using an audience member's phone and told her several things about her life and future that he could not have known without God's insight. She later confirmed that Shawn's prophecy had been wonderfully accurate.

> But when the truth-giving Spirit comes, he will unveil the reality of every truth within you. He won't speak his own message, but only what he hears from the Father, and he will reveal prophetically to you what is to come (John 16:13 TPT).

Dear Lord Jesus, thank You for blessing the world with so many anointed teachers. Please give me discernment to know which ones to follow and support. Give me plenty of opportunities to learn about You, and even to teach others. I want to become confident speaking in front of others in order to influence the world for Your sake. In Your holy name I pray, amen.

Testimonies

It is incredibly helpful to hear someone speak vulnerably about their past, or to read an account of the most frightening, tumultuous, pain-ridden, or humiliating point in someone's life. You can see in these stories how God lifts people up above their circumstances to sit beside Him in a place of healing and restoration. The enemy would have you believe that you're alone in your suffering and that there is no one else who could understand what you're experiencing, but God wants to comfort you with empathy. He will make sure you hear a testimony at the right time in your life so that it speaks directly to you in your pain.

> All you lovers of God who want to please him, come and listen, and I'll tell you what he did for me. I cried aloud to him with all my heart and he answered me! Now my mouth overflows with the highest praise (Psalm 66:16-17 TPT).

I love to read Scripture, apologetics, and other books on faith-based life instruction, but my favorite books to read are memoirs, testimonies, and real-life accounts of the miraculous. Who doesn't love a good miracle story! There are countless stories about people who have been visited by angels or by Jesus, or have been saved, delivered, healed, or restored miraculously. Some even claim to have visited heaven! Many of these stories are centered on the theme of deliverance and they have the ability to infuse hope into what might seem like a hopeless situation. After all, Jesus Christ came to set the captives free!

Christian radio, television, and internet programs regularly broadcast testimonies and book recommendations. There are also many wonderful movies based on true miracle stories. Topics include deliverance from addiction, escape from satanism and cults, stories of healing including regaining fertility, and stories of miracle rescues and survivals. One of my favorite movies is the powerful story of a mother whose prayers saved her nearly-deceased son after he was rescued from a frozen pond. I also love stories where it's obvious God was central to someone's success, even if that person is oblivious to Him. I could curl up with a box of tissue and watch these testimonies all day long!

> And fasten your thoughts on every glorious work of God, praising him always (Philippians 4:8 TPT).

Dear Lord Jesus, thank You for the countless testimonies that strengthen Your church. Please guide me to the best ones for my situation, and give me the opportunity to write my own. I want to hear stories every day about what You've done for others. In Your holy name I pray, amen.

Speak Life

You are powerful when you speak. Your words have the power to make someone's day—or ruin it. When you bless others you also receive a blessing. It's a win-win! Your words are especially powerful for your family and close friends. Tell them who they are in Christ, otherwise they may never know. Remember, people won't remember what car you drove or clothes you wore, but they will remember how your words made them feel and how you inspired them.

> And never let ugly or hateful words come from your mouth, but instead let your words become beautiful gifts that encourage others; do this by speaking words of grace to help them (Ephesians 4:29 TPT).

> Nothing is more appealing than speaking beautiful, life-giving words. For they release sweetness to our souls and inner healing to our spirits (Proverbs 16:24 TPT).

I've been called many fun nicknames, but we've all heard someone say something discouraging about us. Classmates said all sorts of unpleasant things about me as a child—that I was ugly, weird, and vain (this combination doesn't add up, but so it goes with satan's lies). Early on, the enemy used other people to distort my image of myself, which caused me to alter my behavior negatively in order to gain positive responses from other people. I was terrified of being rejected or insulted. I wanted desperately to be accepted, adored, and loved. So as a teenager, I became obsessed with my appearance and pleasing others rather than pleasing God.

Our identities in Christ are priceless and must be protected, just like every gift of God that satan attempts to wreck with his lies. Regardless of how or why things are said to us, words have the power to shape both the opinion we hold of ourselves and who we become. When I speak of others, particularly of my children, my words should be reflective of the good in them and of their destiny. They will stumble along the way, but these will not be occasions to elevate myself over them with words. If I do, they may come to believe that the things I say about them in a temporary moment of weakness are permanently true. If they fall, my words should be like a hand to gently lift them up.

Of the tongue, the Bible instructs us to keep it from evil and deceit (Psalm 34:13); says it is a tree of life when wholesome, but breaks the spirit when perverse (Proverbs 15:4); it promotes health in the wise (Proverbs 12:18); should be guarded to keep the soul from trouble (Proverbs 21:23); and that a gentle one can break a bone (Proverbs 25:15).

> God-lovers make the best counselors. Their words possess wisdom and are right and trustworthy (Psalm 37:30 TPT).

> Respond gently when you are confronted and you'll defuse the rage of another. Responding with sharp, cutting words will only make it worse. Don't you know that being angry can ruin the testimony of even the wisest of men? (Proverbs 15:1 TPT).

> *Dear Lord Jesus, please help me control my words, choosing them carefully to build others up. Let them always be graceful and seasoned with the salt of truth. Help me to be especially careful with what I say to my children so they don't become discouraged. In Your holy name I pray, amen.*

Stand Up for the Weak
and Oppressed

ou're most like Christ when you follow His commands to shepherd and assist the weak, defenseless, voiceless, and poor. He did all these things, and is delighted when you do the same, even in the face of persecution, slander, and opposition. You're called to rock the boat, rattle the establishment, flip some tables over, and speak out against abuses carried out by those in power, regardless of the consequences. Following these commands won't be easy. In fact, you may provoke the ire of oppressors. But be one who cares not what man thinks, but only of what God thinks (Galatians 1:10). By doing so you'll find yourself secure and at peace, even in the midst of the storm (Proverbs 29:25). One day you'll look back with joy as you remember when you did the right things.

> But you are to be a king who speaks up on behalf of the disenfranchised and pleads for the legal rights of the defenseless and those who are dying. Be a righteous king, judging on behalf of the poor and interceding for those most in need (Proverbs 31:8-9 TPT).

I often think of the defenseless, innocent babies in the womb, suffering and dying during abortion procedures. I thank God that some states in the U.S. are taking steps to defund abortion mills and outlaw the practice. In April 2019, abortion at any stage of pregnancy was outlawed in Alabama and criminalized for doctors, except in the case of a medical emergency. Several other states have followed suit with their own abortion restrictions. Under President Trump, our government has rescinded tax dollars for agencies that provide abortions. I pray one day Roe versus Wade will be overturned and all abortions banned.

There are many ways to help defend and speak up for the defenseless in the womb. In 2019, I led a few peaceful protests associated with the Pro-Life Action League. Several times a year this group initiates nationwide anti-abortion activism efforts, inviting hundreds of volunteers to take responsibility for the events at their local venues. We held a candlelight prayer vigil outside an Atlanta abortion mill to remember the unborn, while our kids wrote "Keep Your Baby" on the ground outside in sidewalk chalk. We held signs reading "Abortion Takes a Human Life" on a highway overpass during rush hour. Most recently, we held a memorial service for the unborn at a church, gathering around their abortion memorial to pray, worship, and fellowship.

Imagine a history where all the passersby and outsiders stood up to Hitler and the Third Reich, dared to question his madness and intercede on behalf of those he kidnapped, stole from, tortured, and slaughtered. Let's not look back on our own lives and say, "I didn't do enough!" We are the Lord's hands and feet on earth(1 Corinthians 12:27 TPT).

> Defend the defenseless, the fatherless and the forgotten, the disenfranchised and the destitute. Your duty is to deliver the poor and the powerless; liberate them from the grasp of the wicked (Psalm 82:3-4 TPT).

Dear Lord Jesus, thank You for shining your light on the darkness, revealing where I must take a stand for the helpless and oppressed. Please give me the courage, resources, and relationships I need to carry out Your work. Help me not get discouraged and to stay connected to your power through prayer and worship. In Your holy name I pray, amen.

Create for the Kingdom and Encourage One Another

God has given you creative gifts and ideas to influence people and to grow His kingdom. Your projects and creations are infused with the Holy Spirit, drawing people closer to God through the beauty they see in your work. He gives you fulfilling work that you will eventually master because He has equipped you with the personalized gifts needed to achieve His purposes. Paul had many gifts—preaching, teaching, speaking, and writing. He wrote more of the Bible than any other one person! He was passionate and tireless because the Holy Spirit was working through him.

> I have been made a messenger of this wonderful news by the gift of grace that works through me. Even though I am the least significant of all his holy believers, this grace-gift was imparted when the manifestation of his power came upon me. Grace alone empowers me so that I can boldly preach this wonderful message to non-Jewish people, sharing with them the unfading, inexhaustible riches of Christ, which are beyond comprehension (Ephesians 3:7-8 TPT).

I have been called to write for the kingdom, and have known it since the first time I published a blog post about God. It was exciting and fulfilling to consider how many people were reading about my relationship with Jesus. Writing allows me to reach lost and hurting people I would likely never encounter otherwise. I believe this book is going to encourage new believers who probably have a lot of questions about what it means to follow Christ. I even have ideas for my next book because God has already planted that seed!

When we pursue our calling in Jesus, He will meet our more advanced needs of esteem, independence, self-actualization or mastery of our calling, wealth, and fame (for some). Rather than striving and chasing after these things for their own sake, His instructions are to, "constantly chase after the realm of God's kingdom and the righteousness that proceeds from Him. Then all these less important things will be given to you abundantly" (Matthew 6:33 TPT). Make it your mission to help others and glorify Him through your work, and He will make your cause shine like the dawn.

God also calls us to support and encourage others to create for the kingdom: "Because of this, encourage the hearts of your fellow believers and support one another, just as you have already been doing" (1 Thessalonians 5:11 TPT). I love to see social media posts and read books where a person who deserves to be celebrated themselves is actually celebrating someone else. We don't see this often enough, but it is truly awesome! In lifting up someone else and their accomplishments, we actually lift ourselves up with them.

> Jesus answered, "The work you can do for God starts with believing in the One he has sent" (John 6:29 TPT).

Dear Lord Jesus, thank You for the gifts You've given me to help others and glorify You. Please help me work for Your purposes, not mine, and to chase after Your reward rather than the world's. Also, please give me opportunities to help others identify and develop their gifts and callings. In Your holy name I pray, amen.

Feed His Lambs

At some point, you've probably invested some of your resources in anticipation of growth and return. Have you ever considered that children are the best investment of your time and money? Even if you don't have children of your own, there are plenty you could still help. Children need the basics: food, shelter, and clothing. But they also need spiritual food. They need mentors, someone who will direct them to Christ and show them His love. The return on this investment is invaluable.

> After they had breakfast, Jesus said to Peter, "Simon, son of John, do you burn with love for me more than these?" Peter answered, "Yes, Lord! You know that I have great affection for you!" "Then take care of my lambs," Jesus said. Jesus repeated his question the second time, "Simon, son of John, do you burn with love for me?" Peter answered, "Yes, my Lord! You know that I have great affection for you!" "Then take care of my sheep," Jesus said. Then Jesus asked him again, "Peter, son of John, do you have great affection for me?" Peter was saddened by being asked the third time and said, "My Lord, you know everything. You know that I burn with love for you!" Jesus replied, "Then feed my lambs!" (John 21:15-17 TPT).

One day I opened my Bible to a random page and read something to the effect of, "Dearest woman, I'm glad to see your children are being taught." I can't quote the chapter and verse because it was in the middle of the night, at a time when I was just hungry for God's approval. It could have been in John or James, but I certainly can't find it now. I'd like to think maybe God inserted a personalized note just for me in my dark moment of doubt. I'm not a perfect parent, but that night when I stopped to wonder what God thought, He had only words of encouragement and affirmation for me. He sees our efforts to shepherd the young ones He's entrusted us with— our children. As a good Father, He encourages and kindly corrects us along the way.

As long as we make the effort to feed our children spiritually, God will fight the inevitable battles that arise. We are always up against insecurity, feeling overwhelmed or exhausted, and the occasional disinterest and distraction on the kids' part. So it's important to use what our kids enjoy as a springboard for teaching. Jackson, my eldest, loves comic-style books, including the Bible and children's classics that are illustrated in that style. Charles, a few years younger, loves to learn about Jesus and God's creation from a scientific perspective. We frequently read from Louis Giglio's children's books, which use basic scientific concepts to explain God's love. Evelyn, as a preschooler, loves all kinds of toys and watching their unboxing and demonstration on the adorable Internet video channel, "Growing Little Ones for Jesus." My sweet baby, Nick Jr., has so much fun dancing along with praise and worship music anywhere.

After Jackson completed first grade, we made the tough decision to withdraw him from his lovely private school in favor of homeschooling. I had not considered it seriously until my youngest reached nine to ten months, and I'd made it through the newborn survival fog. I was simply convicted one day that we weren't getting to see Jackson enough! We would spend about fifteen minutes together in the mornings, and after school he was understandably tired, just wanting to decompress in front of the television. Homeschooling has been a wonderful transition, bringing more health, joy, ease, and togetherness into our lives. Let's invite our children to spend their best hours with us.

> Jesus called out to them and said, "Come and follow me, and I will transform you into men who catch people for God." Immediately they dropped their nets and left everything behind to follow Jesus (Matthew 4:19-20 TPT).

Dear Lord Jesus, thank You for the gift of children! We all want to feel loved, and there is no one more loving than a child. Please give me opportunities to help children who need to see and feel Your love. Help me to see them through Your eyes of compassion. In Your holy name I pray, amen.

Find Him in Them

For a long time before I had children, I didn't understand what was meant by God's "presence." You may believe there is a God somewhere in the universe, but perhaps He feels far away, disconnected from you, and indifferent to your worries. How do you find His presence? It's really quite simple. Spend some time with a child. Read and play with them. Ask them questions and gaze into their eyes. Care for them and let them get close to you—and you'll be in God's presence.

> And the King will answer them, "Don't you know? When you cared for one of the least important of these my little ones, my true brothers and sisters, you demonstrated love for me" (Matthew 25:40 TPT).

We took Jackson and Charlie to Hawaii when Charlie was just seven months old. After enduring two six-hour flights to get there that December, we spent two weeks on the Big Island at Christmastime. While we were there, Charlie was dedicated to the Lord and we celebrated Jackson's fourth birthday. The Lord was close to us the entire trip, including the day of Jackson's birthday party when our reservation had been mysteriously deleted. We arrived at the beach to find the picnic shelter we'd reserved already in use by another party for a child of a similar age. Miraculously, her family invited us to join them and even play their party games. It ended up being a blessing having so many additional kids to celebrate with. God never disappoints when it comes time to celebrate, especially for one of his little lambs.

Evy was born nearly a year later. As soon as she arrived, I said, "She's perfect!" She was, and still is, absolutely beautiful. Her voice, hair, skin, facial features, and her laugh are some of the sweetest and most precious things on earth to behold. She's my best friend and I am forever grateful to God for choosing me to be her mommy. Her name means "Little Bird" and birds are often symbolic of angels. I believe our sweet Evy is an angel personified and is heavily guarded by heaven's host.

Nick Jr. is also a miracle baby. Shortly after my water broke on the day he was born, I fainted in the bathroom. I came to on the tile floor resting on my knees and forearms, with no pain. By God's grace, my belly had not hit the floor and Nick was delivered naturally several hours later, arriving in perfect health. He's by far the cuddliest of my babies. While most toddlers want to be on the go, busy as can be, he would be quite content in my arms most of the day. Children are truly the embodiment of Christ's love, as they're quick to forgive, kind, honest, and pure.

> Be careful that you not corrupt one of these little ones. For I can assure you that in heaven each of their angelic guardians have instant access to my heavenly Father (Matthew 18:10 TPT).

> The very next day John saw Jesus coming to him to be baptized, and John cried out, "Look! There he is—God's Lamb! He will take away the sins of the world!" (John 1:29 TPT).

> *Dear Lord Jesus, thank You for the children in my life. Please give me patience and kindness to treat them as I would treat You. Help me remember what it was like to be a child, what I longed for, and the times I felt loved. I want my children to know and follow You all their lives. In Your holy name I pray, amen.*

The Last Will Be First

If you've ever been chosen last—or worse, not chosen at all—you know the sting of rejection. Maybe you've been excluded from a social club or gathering, and it seems you're the only one who didn't get in. Imagine being the person who's never been chosen for anything. Imagine being perpetually rejected, ridiculed, abused, and called a mistake. There are so many like this who the world has cast aside and forgotten, but those same outcasts who belong to Christ will one day be seated beside Him in a place of honor.

> Now you can understand what I meant when I said that the first will end up last and the last will end up being first. Everyone is invited, but few are the chosen (Matthew 20:16 TPT).

Once while on an airplane, I realized the usual process of boarding and exiting a large commercial aircraft is the perfect illustration of Matthew 20:16. Passengers sitting at the rear of the plane, who are typically boarded early, end up exiting last. In Jesus' parable, the workers hired at the end of the day were generously paid for a full day, the same as the workers hired at daybreak. Perhaps the late hires looked too sick, weak, or tired to work a full day, but in the kingdom they are not penalized for their shortcomings and appearances. It seems they actually receive a windfall, as some only work for one hour. God extends grace and generosity to all His servants with a willing heart.

In God's kingdom, the standards of human value and worth are just the opposite of worldly standards. Tim Tebow's prom night events are a beautiful picture of the kingdom reversal. According to his foundation's website, the prom night experience is centered on God's love for teens with special needs.[9] At these events, the young people who would most likely be overlooked during, or more likely absent from, a traditional pageant or school dance are those who are crowned kings and queens.

Child adoption/sponsorship agencies and pregnancy resource centers are also shining examples of God's love in a world that can be harsh and cruel. Those are places where unwanted babies, otherwise considered last and deemed unworthy of life, are loved, valued, and placed with adoptive families who consider them first from then on. Nick and I are blessed to sponsor children through an organization that provides healthcare, education, and basic necessities to children in underdeveloped countries. We write to these girls in Togo and Peru and receive translated letters and photographs in return. We may also get to visit them one day.

> So, you are not foreigners or guests, but rather you are the children of the city of the holy ones, with all the rights as family members of the household of God (Ephesians 2:19 TPT).

> *Dear Lord Jesus, thank You for putting first those the world considers last. Help me find ways to honor and lift them up. Give me Your eyes to see their eternal beauty and worth. In Your holy name I pray, amen.*

---

9. "Night to Shine," Tim Tebow Foundation™ website, accessed October 11, 2019, https://www.timtebowfoundation.org/ministries/night-to-shine#overview.

Afterword

Six years ago when I began this book-writing journey, if someone had told me that I would one day be content, focused, free, and hopeful, I would have smiled politely and thanked them; but I certainly wouldn't have agreed with them or gotten my hopes up for a better existence. At the time, I couldn't have imagined what a better existence might be. I felt that life was something that just happened to a person, and the odds were good that it would mostly be unpleasant. So I was content to have nice stories to write about Jesus and His kindness to fill up the long, meager days. Now I can see the big picture. As soon as I asked Him, God began renewing my mind (Romans 12:2) and leading me toward an unimaginable new reality (1 Cor. 2:9) to ensure a beautiful future for me and my family. My children will face inevitable challenges and heartaches in their lifetimes, but they will never have to wonder about God's goodness and provision. They will always take comfort and strength in the truth about who they are and who they were created to serve.

It is believed that while on earth, Jesus performed many more miracles than those recorded in the Bible. I began writing this book in 2014, and truthfully, I'm having difficulty wrapping it up now in 2020 because I want to add a new story about God's love each day. The beauty of His wonder and mercies can't be expressed in a single work. For example, my family recently returned home from a lovely winter beach trip. From the details of our room number (7) and welcome gifts, to the beautiful rainbow and tandem-rotor helicopter fly-over framing the sky as we stepped onto the beach, the Lord's hand was blissfully evident the entire time. He is there in every precious detail. The first eatery we visited was a bakery staffed by a lady with Down Syndrome who blessed us all with a hug. Another employee there was able to engage my sons with his impressive knowledge of a hugely-popular galactic battle movie saga and photographs of his figurine collection from the movie series. We enjoyed good weather and didn't suffer any vacation mishaps. We were blessed and cared for every moment of the trip, as if God had ordered each of our steps (Psalm 37:23)!

As I prepare to publish my first book independently, without the help of a publishing company, I can't help but feel a bit underqualified and nervous. Each time I work on the title setup process on the distributor website, my stomach begins to turn. I'm terrified of making a mistake! But then God reassures me. He says, "Move forward and I will help you." He says, "Do not be afraid, for I am with you." He gives me the encouragement I need to advance a little each day. When I struggled with naming the book, He confirmed the title selection with a devotional email that included a beautiful reminder of what it means to be His child. After my editor completed the final round of edits I requested, the new page count came to 170. I then experienced overwhelming peace and contentment with the manuscript because God uses the number seventy to represent perfect spiritual order. I believe He inspired this book and placed it in your hands to impart wisdom and encouragement because He delights in you, His child. Won't you embrace Him as your adoring Father?

About the Author

Samantha Harrell has been writing about the great love of our Lord Jesus since she was thirty, when she began accumulating stories about her encounters with Him. Her prophetic aunt told her then that the Lord said to write down all the miraculous things she was experiencing—dreams, visions, and angelic encounters. So in 2014, she started a blog titled, "Under God's Wings," which eventually became the inspiration for this book. She began compiling the book in 2018 when another prophetic friend shared, "The Lord says, 'It's time to write.'"

Samantha loves Jesus, her family, and babies—including those still enjoying the womb. As an advocate for the unborn, she works to humanize and protect life at all stages, praying and anticipating the end of abortion in our nation. Samantha lives in Atlanta, Georgia, with her husband, Nicholas, their four homeschooled children, and a cat named Bonnie.

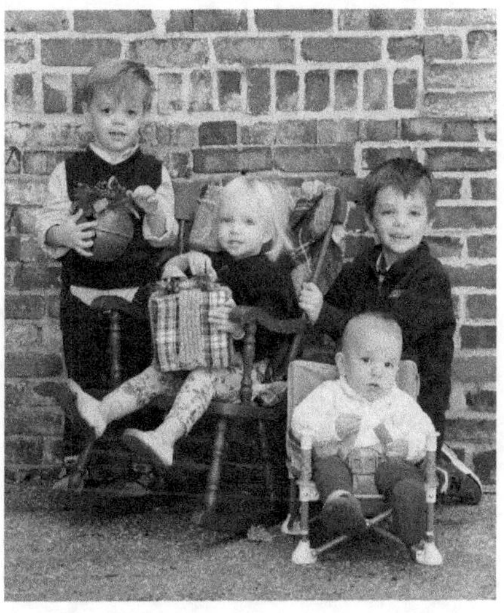

Follow her following Him:
https://www.facebook.com/samantha.harrell.9
https://www.instagram.com/samantha.c.harrell
https://undergodswings.wordpress.com
Contact: samantha_harrell@icloud.com